Dedicated to the lawless rabble.

People's Histreh
Nottingham & Notts Radical History Group

Nottingham Rising

The Great Cheese Riot of 1766 & the 1831 Reform Riots

Valentine Yarnspinner

Loaf On A Stick Press
Nottingham

Nottingham Rising

The Great Cheese Riot of 1766
& the 1831 Reform Riots

Valentine Yarnspinner

Published by

LOAF ON A STICK PRESS

www.peopleshistreh.wordpress.com
peopleshistreh@riseup.net

Nottingham, October 2014
Reprinted June 2015

ISBN 9780956913968

Original pamphlets *To the Castle!...* and *Damn his Charity...* first published in 2010 and 2011.

Printed by
ImprintDigital.com

Acknowledgements

We owe thanks to many people who continue to help us with our projects. There are of course the librarians at the Local Studies Library, the archivists at Nottinghamshire Archives, the University of Nottingham's Manuscripts and Special Collections department, as well as at the National Archives (may all their budgets never be cut). We also want to express our gratitude to those working and volunteering at that marvellous hidden gem right in Nottingham city centre, Bromley House Library.

We very much thank all our comrades, friends and families who have supported us in many ways, especially by being very patient with us.[1] We are also very grateful to all the booksellers and stallholders who agreed to flog our stuff, as well as all those individuals and groups who have advertised and supported our activities, especially our friends from the Nottingham Women's History Group.[2]

Of course we owe much gratitude to all those researchers and writers without whose books and papers we would not even have been able to start the projects resulting in this little book. Special thanks must go to Richard Gaunt from the University of Nottingham, whose extensive and meticulous work, especially with the Duke of Newcastle's diaries, has proved to be invaluable as well as highly entertaining. Richard has also repeatedly done an excellent performance of Newcastle's words during our guided walks 'To the Castle!'.

Indeed, it is our many friends' and comrades' awesome and powerful performances that bring these events to life, so thanks to everyone who has helped with our walks, especially Colin for his passionate contributions, gleefully voiced with the perfect local twang.

Finally, we would very much like to thank you, the reader who picked up this book and all the people who come to our talks and events. We continue to be delighted as well as astounded by how many people have joined us over the years in commemorating all those who stirred things up over the course of the city's and county's turbulent history. You keep us motivated to keep on digging for weird and wonderful, but also tragic and infuriating stories from our tumultuous past.

---

1 Given that 'To a Worm in Horseradish, the World is Horseradish', many an enthusiastic researcher has tested her/his peers' patience with going on just a little bit too much about their respective project.

2 Please see www.nottinghamwomenshistory.org.uk for further information on the NWHG group and their current program of talks and guided walks.

Contents

Foreword to this edition

Writing a foreword is a weird and daunting thing to do. Ideally you get a clever and well respected person to praise your work. Alternatively you write something deep yet catchy yourself, allowing the reader to dive into the subject matter with a smile on their face and well-chosen words of wisdom resonating in their mind. If you expect either of that, better skip this passage now and just get on with the book.

We, the People's Histreh group, are a small circle of friends, united also by a shared passion for history and a deeply felt aversion to the past and present state of power and production relations dominating our society, as well as revulsion for those upholding or trying to change them for the worse. A few years ago, a memorable event with the late Ray Gosling at Nottingham's fabulous Sparrows' Nest[3] eventually led to us meeting up every now and then to eat significant amounts of cake, and share more or less odd nuggets of amazing local history. A history made by many courageous women and men, confronted with incredible hardship and brutal repression, engaging in inspiring acts of direct action as well as organising themselves and their communities in efforts to change their lives for the better. Indeed, as stated on all our leaflets, Nottingham and Nottinghamshire have a long and turbulent history of social and economic transformation, disturbance and conflict. There is a lot to be unearthed and the most amazing, inspiring, shocking and outrageous stories leap out wherever the surface is scratched.

Two of these stories are being (re-)told in this book. We first published them a few years ago as two little pamphlets and to our delight and surprise they proved so popular that we had to reprint them a couple of times. Following our success in publishing Chris Richardson's most excellent book *A City of Light...*[4] last year (which has since been reprinted twice!), and faced again by depleted stocks we thought it was time to reissue the pamphlets in a paperback edition.

Republishing our depictions and interpretations of Nottingham's Great Cheese Riot of 1766 and the 1831 Reform Riots, we got rid of a few errors (whilst undoubtedly adding quite a few more), rearranged tables, maps and illustrations. We also rechecked, rewrote and added a few bits and bobs and allowed one Radical Histerian to go on a wild quest hunting down layout inconsistencies and spending much time moving tables back and forth in half millimetre steps (chores that can never be completed).

---

3 The Sparrows' Nest, a centre for anarchist culture and education, is primarily an archive and library for anarchist/left libertarian materials, including many rare or even unique documents (www.thesparrowsnest.org.uk).

4 Richardson, Christopher (2013): *A City of Light: Socialism, Chartism and Co-operation – Nottingham 1844*; Loaf On A Stick Press; Nottingham.

We hope you enjoy this book and very much hope you will come to one of our future events, walks, etc. And just to prove that we do not (only) repeat and republish time and again what we have done in years past, please keep an eye on our (very irregularly updated) online presence where you will find new materials and information on new projects, event announcements, etc.

As ever, if you spot some errors or would like to comment or contribute additional information, please get in touch (peopleshistreh@riseup.net).

Sincerely yours

Valentine Yarnspinner/the People's Histreh group

Nottingham
October 2014

Damn his Charity!

Contextualising Nottingham's Great Cheese Riot of 1766

Introduction

> *'[In October 1766] Goose Fair was the occasion of a "great cheese riot" [...]. Stalls were attacked and ransacked, and cheeses distributed to the crowd. Being barrel-shaped they could easily be rolled, and soon they were being propelled down Wheeler Gate and Peck Lane. The mayor, trying desperately to intervene, stood in the middle of Peck Lane, only to be knocked over by an accelerating cheese.'*[5]

This tale of the Great Cheese Riot has been (re-)told in many accounts of Nottingham's history[6] and caught my attention primarily as it conjures up entertaining images of modern day local politicians involved in such a classic slapstick scene.

Furthermore, members of the People's Histreh group have on various occasions carried loaves of bread on sticks around, thereby reviving what by the turn of the nineteenth century had become a well-established signal to start a Food Riot.[7] Obviously we could not keep up this habit without examining Nottingham's most famous Food Riot, although it quickly became apparent that no loaves on sticks were reported to have been carried aloft during any of the examined riots.

When research began into the wider story behind the tale, there was no specific interest in the subject other than the intention to discover some further information. After the initial examination of a number of issues of *The Leicester and Nottingham Journal* (hereafter *Journal*) from 1766, two theses were outlined: firstly, it appeared that the riot in Nottingham was just one event in a series of Food Riots in September and October 1766, and secondly, that these events were not only less jolly but also more complex affairs than implied by the standard references to the Great Cheese Riot, which usually depict the riot as an anti-social version of the popular sport of Cheese-Rolling.

---

5 Beckett (b); pp. 287-8.
6 See e.g. Bryson; p. 129.
7 Thompson; p. 70.

In order to examine these theses I took a closer look at the Great Cheese Riot itself before contextualising it with other riotous events described in the *Journal*, asking whether it is possible to identify recurring patterns of the rioters' direct action, as well as how their contemporaries responded to and interpreted these events.

Aside from the *Journal* issues, a number of standard volumes on the history of Nottingham, such as Deering's *The History of Nottingham* or the *Date Book*, were used. Among other works consulted were titles such as the *Cambridge Economic History* and Thompson's *The Making of the English Working Class*. One of the revelations of this research process was to discover that historical dictionaries are treasure troves of information, proving to be highly beneficial for instance in debating the depictions of the rioters.

A few deliberations regarding my attitude towards historical research, the used sources, and my bias of tending to side with the rioters, are followed in the second chapter by a description of the Great Cheese Riot. The events in Nottingham are contextualised and discussed in the third chapter, starting with my definition of Food Riots and some other general deliberations on the subject, before identifying and debating recurring patterns of rioters' direct action as well as the immediate response of their opponents. The fourth chapter focuses on attempts of preventative appeasement, which were made on a number of levels in order to stop further rioting. A passage discussing recurring patterns of the depiction of rioters by their contemporaries, as well as scattered hints regarding their identities, is followed by the sixth chapter focussing on interpretations of price developments and the rioters' motives.

1. Cake and Orwell

It is crucial to urge the reader to be critical of, and highly vigilant towards, any of the deliberations in this book. History is always written by people and people have preconceived ideas, political opinions etc. I cannot provide you with an objective and/or truthful account of events; indeed I strongly believe that no such thing can be done. Instead I offer an interpretation of other people's documentation of past events, whilst providing readers with the information necessary to retrace the research process for themselves.

I can draw an analogy (always a dangerous thing to do) between the research process resulting in a book like this one and baking a cake. A baker has to decide which cake to bake and then to start rummaging for suitable utensils and ingredients deemed necessary for that specific cake, leaving aside other things you would need for different cakes. Although it is the baker who will actually be baking the cake, the preconditions of that process require the involvement of many other persons.

Bakers (as well as researchers), although themselves weighing and combining (analysing and interpreting) ingredients (sources/data), do so utilising a recipe, units of measurement and utensils (theoretical concepts/methodology) that are chosen by, but usually do not originate with, the baker. And just as bakers (usually) do not lay eggs or mill wheat, sources used by researchers are pieces of information which were recorded by other persons in particular ways for particular reasons. Therefore cakes, as well as research projects, are determined by numerous and variable decisions (starting with the very decision to bake a cake), whilst complex preconditions form the basis of such an undertaking. It is not only the sources, but also the researcher's individual circumstances, opinions and experiences that shape the research process, putting into perspective explicit or implicit claims of historians being able to offer objective accounts. To be aware of and to admit this does not negate a scientific approach, but must be the basis of any such claim.

This text is primarily based on five issues of the *Journal*. Reverting to the cake analogy, working with these sources could be compared to using a pre-prepared cake mix rather than a number of separate ingredients. The newspaper issues are edited compilations of articles from other papers, official proclamations, letters from a number of persons providing accounts of riots or explanations for the events, etc.

The advantage is that within a single source it is possible to find evidence contributed by a number of very different people, writing for different reasons, sometimes complementing, sometimes contradicting each other. However, it is crucial to remember that this information was edited according to the editors' agenda and it can be assumed that this was primarily determined by an interest to sell the paper. For example the prominence of the riots and the alarmist language in many articles does not necessarily imply that the rioters were a real threat to power and production relations in Britain. It reflects, at least in part, an editorial choice based on the assumption that riots are exciting and that exciting news sell newspapers. Clive Emsley refers to a pattern of increased reports of crime during peacetime, an observation which may also be assumed to be valid with regards to the reporting of riotous disturbances. The riots of 1766 happened in the aftermath of the Seven Years' War, i.e. at a time when '[...] newspapers found themselves with space to fill because of a decline in exciting [...] war news'.[8] Indeed, the *Journal* issues did feature not only many accounts of riots, but also quite detailed stories about gruesome murders and, as news about domestic unrest became sparse in the issue dated 1st November, a lengthy report of a trial of rioters in New York.[9]

It seems likely that the reports of the riots of autumn 1766 had been spiced up to a certain extent, making it necessary to be highly suspicious for instance of information specifying details such as numbers of rioters or amounts of goods expropriated. Furthermore, although the *Journal* did report extensively on riotous disturbances, the documentation of the individual events is sometimes fragmentary and repeatedly based on second or even third hand reports. Many of these deliberations would therefore greatly benefit from being validated through further research and are at present based on circumstantial evidence only.

In spite of these problems, making it necessary to treat the information provided with great care, the *Journal* issues are wonderful sources, not least because of their language and things like adverts for 'Powders for Disorders in Children'.[10]

Furthermore this research project did not so much aim to reconstruct single events, aside from the Great Cheese Riot itself, but rather to identify and discuss patterns of (direct) action(s), reactions as well as riot-related discourse. The quantity of information provided by the *Journal* issues alone makes it possible to initiate such an undertaking, though it must be done in a very cautious way.

As to the problem of the researcher, i.e. me, consciously or unconsciously sympathising with certain historical protagonists, I have to admit that my immediate reaction to this and to similar subject matters can be summed up with George Orwell's words:

> 'I have no particular love for the idealized "worker" as he appears in the bourgeois Communist's mind, but when I see an

---

8 Emsley; p. 35.

9 See *Journal*; 4th October 1766; p. 1; 1st November 1766; p. 4.

10 *Journal*; 4th October 1766; p. 2.

> actual flesh-and-blood worker in conflict with his natural enemy, the policeman, I do not have to ask myself which side I am on.'[11]

This bias is not only reflected by the subject matter itself, but also in my approach to it and the language used. This is however less of a problem as long as I stay aware of the very real possibility that many rioters may have been bigoted, racist, homophobic misogynists. I also need to constantly strive to remain vigilant not to glorify and idealise any social struggles, especially as the 'flesh-and-blood workers' can turn out to be just as despicable as 'the policeman' they are fighting.

11 Orwell; p. 109.

2. Nottingham's Great Cheese Riot

Although still dominated by agriculture,[12] by the year 1766 England was already in the early stages of what was to become known as the Industrial Revolution, the essence of which Eric Hobsbawm brilliantly summarised as the (still ongoing) process by which 'revolutionary change became the norm'.[13]

Revolutionary changes, gathering pace at an increasing rate, therefore had already started to transform urban as well as rural areas[14] and had also begun to take effect in Nottingham. The town's staple trades, the textile industries, were already well established. It has been estimated that by 1770 the number of merchant hosiers had doubled[15] since the early 1740s.[16] Though the canal, vital to transform the town into a centre of mass production, was not opened until the end of the eighteenth century,[17] the rivers Trent and Leen already provided the town with a favourable infrastructure.

Nottingham's population had steadily increased in the thirty years after 1739 from c.10,000[18] to c.15,000, a significant, though still slow rise if compared to the explosive growth which was to occur by the end of the century.[19]

The scenery of the town, which had previously been described as 'Fair Nottingham with brilliant Beauty graced', a place full of 'Health, Plenty, Pleasure'[20] was beginning to change. Although in the 1760s Nottingham resembled not yet what would later be described as a 'mighty prison of

---

12 Pinchbeck; p. 7.

13 Hobsbawm (b); p. 29.

14 May; pp. 26-33. See Beckett (a); pp. 1-10: Beckett provides a partial summary of the debates whether or not these transformations amount to an agricultural revolution. See Brenner; p. 68; Rich/Wilson (a); pp. 275-9/299-301: A number of developments in the agricultural sector, e.g. enclosures, the decline of small landowners and small tenancies, innovations to increase production etc. can be traced into the seventeenth and earlier centuries. However, after 1750 these processes occurred on an unprecedented scale.

15 Beckett (b); p. 317.

16 Deering; p. 101: He estimated around 1,200 frames were in use in c.1740.

17 Kayne; pp. 88-9. See *Journal* 25th October 1766; p. 1: Complex canal systems were already operational in other parts of Britain, such as in Manchester, which was said to have 'become a sort of a maritime town'.

18 Deering; pp. 12-3.

19 Beckett (b); p. 191: According to Beckett, the town's population increase spiralled in the 1780s by more than forty per cent, i.e. the population grew from 17,200 to 24,400. See *To the Castle!* ...; chapter 1.2.: By the beginning of the 1830s, 50,000 persons inhabited the same area where c.10,000 had lived a century before. Before 1845 the town grew only in population, not in area.

20 Deering; p. 17.

brick and mortar',[21] the years between 1763-8 saw the first considerable building boom. Within the next two decades the town would no longer be dominated by the 'fine houses' of 'gentlemen of great fortune' but rather by slums consisting of the notorious back-to-back houses.[22] Within less than two generations, the transformation of Nottingham would result in atrocious living and working conditions on an unprecedented scale for the vast majority of its inhabitants, also stirring up unparalleled levels of radical dissent and riotous upheaval, earning the town a reputation for being inhabited by a 'combustible' populace.[23]

Thursday, the 2nd October 1766 saw the beginning of the annual Goose Fair in what is now known as Old Market Square. It is reported to have been 'a fine day' and the fair was well attended. Large quantities of cheese were on sale, more than in than previous years, priced between 24s and 36s per hundredweight, which was 'deemed highly excessive'.[24]

However, during the day trading is said to have commenced without disturbances. Events apparently became tense in the evening when 'some rude lads' challenged several Lincolnshire traders who had purchased up to 'sixty hundred [weights] of cheese'. The traders were 'threatened they should not stir a cheese till the town was first served'. According to the *Journal*, they applied for protection, 'but it was not then to be had'. At about 7pm:

> '[...] the mob began to be outrageous, fell upon the heaps of cheese, and amidst loud shouts in a short time took and destroyed the whole parcel, which was chiefly carried off by women and boys.'[25]

According to the *Date Book*:

> 'The people were so exasperated that their violence broke loose like a torrent; cheeses were rolled down Wheeler-gate and Peck-lane in abundance, many others were carried away, and the Mayor, in endeavouring to restore peace, was knocked down with one in the open fair.'[26]

---

21 Bryson; p. 84. For a more detailed depiction of living and working conditions of the industrial Nottingham see *To the Castle!* ...; chapters 1.3.-1.4.

22 Beckett (b); pp. 189/200-1.

23 See *To the Castle!* ...; chapter 1.1./Appendix XIV.

24 Field; Vol. 2; p. 69; *Journal*; 11th October 1766; p. 3.

25 Ibid.

26 Field; Vol. 2; p. 69. This indicates that contrary to the common tale of the Cheese Riot the mayor may not have been bowled over in Peck Lane but knocked down with a cheese on Market Square, which is not quite as entertaining but still rather funny.

Probably encouraged by the successful expropriations and the fun of bowling over/knocking down gentlemen, an unknown number of people left the town centre and went down to the River Trent to search the warehouses situated near the bridges, before returning again after 'finding no cheese' there. Two or three persons were arrested and 'carried before the Justices', apparently in a 'Coffee House' in Peck Lane (an alleyway linking Market Square and St Peter's Gate), which became the crowd's next target. The arrests had 'redoubled their fury' and the rioters were determined to liberate the prisoners:

> '[...] they broke the windows belonging to the house, tore the pavement and threatened destruction to all who opposed them: It was thought prudent to discharge the lads in custody and then [the rioters] retreated.'[27]

Later that night the effectively helpless 'civil powers' of Nottingham sent a messenger to Derby to request military support and in the early hours of the next morning, cavalry and infantry units arrived.[28]

During the day the atmosphere was 'very peaceable', before a second riot broke out in the evening, 'more dangerous than the former'. There were serious clashes between rioters and military 'at the New-change'.[29] The troops apparently acted with 'great vigour in quelling the tumult, which was not fully subdued until blood had been shed'. The soldiers repeatedly discharged their firearms into the crowds. Their only victim known by name was William Egglestone, 'a farmer, at Carcolston near Bingham'. He was shot through the calf of his right leg 'as he was kneeling and leaning over a heap of cheese'. The wound infected and he died the following Sunday. An inquest into his death came to the conclusion of 'Accidental Death, [caused] by a Person [...] unknown'.[30] This verdict was not quite as cynical as it first appears, as Egglestone apparently was not shot whilst trying to expropriate, but rather whilst 'guarding' the cheese, which makes the incident a case of friendly fire. Other persons are said to have been wounded by the soldiers' fire, but neither of the used sources provide any further information on their injuries or whether they recovered from them.[31]

Eventually the crowds dispersed, but a number of persons again went to Trent Bridge where they seized a boat 'laden with cheese.' On Saturday, people 'behaved very insolently to the Magistrates' who deemed it necessary

---

27 *Journal*; 11th October 1766; p. 3.

28 Ibid. See Field; Vol. 2; pp. 69-70: The soldiers were part of a regiment called the 'Fifteenth Dragoons (formed out of the Duke of Kingston's Light Horse)'.

29 *Journal*; 11th October 1766; p. 3. See Nottingham City Council: The New Change stood on the site where the Council House was built in the late 1920s.

30 *Journal*; 11th October 1766; p. 3.

31 Field; Vol. 2; p. 70.

to read the Riot Act. On Monday, a party of soldiers marched out of the town to confront rioters who were rumoured to have gathered near Derby to destroy a warehouse. The same evening the Great Cheese Riot finally came to an end after several hundred people tried to burn a windmill near Trent Bridge, but:

> '[...] they retreated from thence, without doing any considerable damage, on the report of the Magistrates and soldiers coming to defend it, which they did soon after their departure.'[32]

[32] *Journal*; 11th October 1766; p. 3.

3. Patterns of direct action

For Thompson, Food Riots were the 'most common example' of what he called 'more or less spontaneous popular direct action',[33] as any 'sharp' increase in food prices 'precipitated riot'. He assumed that Food Riots demonstrated 'more sophisticated traditions than the word 'riot' suggests.' Therefore an examination of the reports on the 1766 Food Riots should reveal recurring patterns of the rioters' direct action, indicating that the riots were indeed more than 'a mere uproar which culminated in the breaking open of barns or the looting of shops.'[34]

One of the first results was that using the term Food Riots can be misleading. Although some of the food-related unrest reported in the *Journal* issues were indeed significant clashes with a number of fatalities, many others can hardly be described as a 'riot', a term conjuring up images of pitched street battles. For instance, on Saturday, 4th October 1766 an 'old woman' in Ashby-de-la-Zouch 'rubb'd a pound of the butter all over [a farmer's] face' after she was greatly vexed by the price he demanded. Afterwards an 'inconsiderable mob' searched a warehouse for cheese, but soon dispersed when none was to be found. About three weeks later, a small crowd of people stopped a waggon-load of flour in Northamptonshire, which however was 'at length suffered to pass without receiving any damage'.[35]

These examples make it apparent that in many instances Food Riots were actually quite harmless, leaving not only people, but also property unharmed. However, as it is not only quite catchy but also widely used, I decided to use the term in a very broad sense.

Therefore I describe as a Food Riot any event reported on in the examined *Journal* issues, in which direct action (whether riotous or not) was taken by more than one person in order to procure food for personal consumption or for not-for-profit distribution, excluding occurrences which fit the latter category but in which food was obtained by propertied persons and local officials to be distributed or sold at reduced rates as a measure of preventative appeasement (see 4.1).

---

33 Thompson; p. 67: This idea of spontaneous crowd action is opposed to what is commonly understood as the actions of a 'mob'; i.e. 'the deliberate use of the crowd as an instrument of pressure, by persons above or apart from the crowd'. This understanding of a 'mob', manipulated and/or directed by a single or a small number of ringleaders, has been used by historians, 'too often [...] lazily, to evade further analysis, or (with the suggestion of criminal elements motivated by the desire for loot) as a gesture of prejudice.' See also *To the Castle!* ...; chapter 4.1.

34 Thompson; pp. 67-8.

35 See *Journal*; 11th October 1766; p. 3; 18th October 1766; p. 1; 25th October 1766; p. 3.

Based on this definition, the examined *Journal* issues report on a total of twenty-two Food Riots,[36] which occurred in fourteen different counties[37] in England,[38] between the 9th September and the 23rd October 1766.[39]

Bearing in mind that information taken from the *Journal* is often fragmentary and highly questionable, these numerous accounts of Food Riots allow a cautious debate of recurring patterns of rioters' direct actions as well as of the reactions by the rioters' diverse opponents.

3.1. Enforcement of price reductions

In a number of the Food Riots reported in the *Journal*, crowds enforced price reductions, be it directly or indirectly.

Events on Saturday, 18th October 1766 in Gloucestershire, an area dominated by cloth production, are a distinct example of the former category in which people directly regulated prices they deemed excessive. The relatively detailed report in the *Journal* depicted the rioters in a rather typical way:[40]

---

36 See Appendix II. See *Journal*; 11th October 1766; p. 3; *Journal*; 18th October; p. 3: Two riots in Hinckley are not counted in this number of twenty-two, though they are referred to in this text. These broke out after a number of persons were arrested following a Food Riot in the town (no further information could be found regarding the events that preceded these arrests). See also *Journal*; 1st November 1766; p. 3: This issue refers to rumours of another riot in Norwich but this information remains unconfirmed and is therefore also not counted in the aforementioned number. Events in Nuneaton (see 3.1.) demonstrate that the definition above leaves a grey area. Prices were reduced on that occasion before any direct action had been taken, but unlike in other situations when this was done as a measure of preventative appeasement (see 4.1.), propertied persons in Nuneaton only acted when confronted with two hundred colliers. These had already taken things into their own hands the previous day in Coventry and were ready to do so again. Therefore events in that town were counted as a Food Riot. See *Journal* 18th October 1766; p. 1: It is very likely that there were far more instances of Food Riots, as there were e.g. reports of repeated 'riots and disturbances' in 'Oxford and Woodstock', the latter not being mentioned elsewhere in the *Journal* issues.

37 See *Journal*; 4th/11th/18th/25th October; 1st November 1766: Buckinghamshire, Derbyshire, Gloucestershire, Leicestershire, Norfolk, North Yorkshire, Northamptonshire, Nottinghamshire, Oxfordshire, Somerset, Warwickshire, West Midlands, Wiltshire, Worcestershire.

38 See *Journal*; 25th October 1766; p. 1: It can be assumed that at the same time Food Riots occurred in other parts of the British Isles. There were reports of serious crop failures as well as significant exports of wheat from Ireland, a volatile mixture which probably resulted in rioting (see chapters 3.3./4.1.).

39 See *Journal*; 4th/11th/18th/25th October; 1st November 1766; Appendix II.

40 See chapter 5; see also *To the Castle! ...*; chapter 4.

> '[In the area live] a great number of desolate, idle fellows, that delight more in drinking than work: four of these sort of people being assembled together at Pitchcomb feast, and there getting drunk, were the first who kindled the flame of disturbance here; these incendiaries communicating their mad resolutions to others like themselves, and giving out that it was their intention to regulate the prices of victuals as well as drink, assumed to themselves the name of Regulators [...].'[41]

Eventually, a number of 'sturdy young fellows', seized 'several tons' of cheese and sold it at a guinea a hundred weight, about two thirds of the original asking price. Furthermore:

> '[...] bacon, butter, and other commodities, were sold in like manner: by compulsion were the people obliged to part with their several commodities, at prices greatly beneath their real worth.'[42]

On Friday, 26th September two hundred colliers took similar direct action in Coventry. Seizing cheese from a number of warehouses, it was brought into the market and 'a good deal [...] sold by the lump' for a price 2d to 2½d per pound. After the money was handed over to the former owners of the cheese, there was a small 'fray' with 'peace officers', but no arrests or injuries were reported.[43]

Crowds of people directly enforcing price reductions and passing the revenue on to the former owners of the commodities were a recurring pattern of direct action in the 1766 Food Riots. For Thompson, such examples were a sign of the rioters 'self-discipline'.[44] However, the examined sample of Food Riots indicates that this pattern of direct action should not be over-emphasised as it was reported in only four cases, i.e. less than a fifth of all riots. However, in a further fifth of the riots direct action or the mere threat of it was indirectly successful in enforcing price reductions which were organised by local officials.

One example for this occurred in Nuneaton, the aforementioned colliers' target on the day after their successful direct action in Coventry. Their presence and possibly news of events in Coventry motivated local gentlemen to take pre-emptive action in order to prevent the colliers from taking matters into their own hands (again). Therefore a Sir Roger Newdigate ordered 'some hundred weight of his own cheese to be sold at

---

41 *Journal*; 25th October 1766; p. 3.

42 Ibid.

43 *Journal*; 4th October 1766; p. 3. See Hobsbawm (a); p. 59: Apparently there are numerous examples of eighteenth century miners taking direct action 'against high food-prices, and the profiteers believed to be responsible for them'.

44 Thompson; pp. 69-71: This pattern of direct action is also key to Thompson's interpretation of the riots. See chapter 6.

the market there at two pence halfpenny per pound' whilst several farmers brought wheat into the market, 'a thing not seen there for several years past.' In Oxford riots initiated action from local officials, who organised the collection and sale not only of foodstuffs like bread, bacon, cheese and butter, but also commodities like candles and soap, all sold at rates a quarter or even a third lower than the original asking price. Similar events occurred in Birmingham and Norwich where, following serious rioting in September, in October the populace was 'pacified' in this manner.[45]

However, price reductions organised by local officials were not guaranteed to succeed in appeasing riotous or potentially riotous crowds. The strategy failed for example during Food Riots in Leicester[46] or in Derbyshire, where a trader tried to appease a crowd of people who were busy expropriating cheese from a boat, following several days of intense fighting (see 3.5.):

> 'Fifty-Pounds was offer'd by the owner of the cheese, if [the rioters] would suffer the cargos of the boats to remain untouch'd, and that a pair of scales should be erected, and the country supplied at 2d per lb. To which one of the ringleaders replied, Damn his Charity, we'll have the Cheese for nought.'[47]

3.2. Expropriations

Straightforward expropriations such as in Derbyshire were a far more common pattern of direct action than enforcing price reductions, being reported in three out of five accounts of Food Riots. Commodities were expropriated from boats, waggons and carts, market stalls, warehouses[48] or directly from production facilities, for instance a grain mill near Oxford:

> 'Men, Woman, and Children [...] proceeded to Holiwell-mill, from whence [...] they removed one hundred and twenty sacks of flour; all which was [...] loaded upon the miller's cart, and drawn by themselves from thence up to Carfax and there given away among the populace.'[49]

In Leicester expropriations went on in spite of efforts to organise a controlled sale at reduced prices and a significant military presence. Rioting had erupted after a load of cheese was stopped from being carted out of town (see 3.3) and the cheese on the waggon had been distributed 'whole

45 *Journal*; 4th October 1766; pp. 1/3; 11th October 1766; p. 4; 18th October 1766; p. 4.
46 *Journal*; 4th October 1766; p. 3.
47 *Journal*; 11th October 1766; p. 3.
48 *Journal*; 4th October 1766; p. 3; 11th October 1766; p. 3.
49 *Journal*; 4th October 1766; p. 1.

before the Magistrates received any Information of these proceedings'. Afterwards rioting quickly spread through the town despite a large troop of infantry having been mobilised almost instantly. A large amount of cheese, which had been stashed in a pub, was expropriated and a number of stores and warehouses searched. In the evening, groups of rioters began to systematically search waggons going in and out of the town in order to discover further provisions, and were able to expropriate further commodities before the military could intervene. A number of rioters 'remain'd all night in the streets, watching the ends of the town for loaded carriages &c.'[50]

3.3. Stopping the export of provisions

Another recurring pattern were attempts to stop provisions being removed from a market, a town or a county, for example when they were loaded on a boat or a waggon at the end of a market day. In the Food Riots reported in the *Journal* issues, this was repeatedly the trigger for unrest. This indicates a strong conviction amongst rioters that the export of provisions for example from their village, would cause or increase scarcity and push up prices even further.[51]

Even the suspicion of the export of provisions could spark riots, as reported from Coventry:

> '[The rioters'] principal design was to visit the cheese-factors, who, they were persuaded, by engrossing and sending out of the country that commodity, had occasioned it to be at the present exorbitant price.'[52]

This appears to have been well known to traders like John Moore, from Sapcote near Hinckley, who published a note in the *Journal*:

> 'I beg leave to assure the Publick, that I never in my Life Exported any Cheese or purchas'd any by Commission for that purpose.'[53]

That the export of provisions could spark serious riots was also known to local authorities, who were on occasion keen to stop any such enterprise or at least tried to delay it, both on national (see chapter 4.) and local levels. The waggon-load of cheese which started the Leicester riot had been bought by a cheese trader from Market Harborough who consulted the local Magistrates as to whether they thought it prudent to move it. He eventually

---

50 Ibid.; p. 3.

51 See Thompson; p. 68: This appears to contradict Thompson's assumption that the laws of '[...] supply and demand, whereby scarcity inevitably led to soaring prices, had by no means won acceptance in the popular mind.'

52 *Journal*; 4th October 1766; p. 3.

53 *Journal*; 11th October 1766; p. 2.

decided to go ahead with this contrary to their advice, triggering the riot as the waggon was stopped by 'several women', some of whom 'seiz'd the [...] horse by the head, whilst others got into the waggon' and started to distribute the cheese.[54] Other Food Riots started similarly, for example in Warwickshire,[55] or in and around Oxford:

> 'The Disorders occasioned by the late scandalous exportation of grain, at a time when bread as well as all other kind of provisions bear so exorbitant a price, have also broke[n] out in this City. Late on Tuesday night last, an alarm being given that a Waggon load of wheat flour was loaded [...] in order to be privately removed in the Dead of night [...].'[56]

Thompson refers to similar events, stating this as an indicator of 'something in the nature of a war between the countryside and the town', in which people in rural areas were afraid that after corn had been sent to supply towns and cities, they 'would be left to starve'. This, along with farmers' fears of transporting provisions in case they would be seized, and attempts by local authorities trying to appease their populace by maintaining a local stock of grains, apparently repeatedly led to situations when the transport of supplies in Britain could scarcely be maintained.[57]

3.4. Smashing up property

Apart from acquiring provisions, venting anger against those perceived as contributing to, or being, profiteers of high prices, was apparently a priority of many rioters. For Thompson this pattern of direct action showed that even in those 'uproarious' riots, motives were 'more complex than hunger'. Though there are no accounts of crowds attacking for example merchants, grocers, bakers or millers themselves – unless these actively participated in fights with rioters (see 3.5.) – their property was repeatedly targeted during attacks that appear to have sometimes been rather ferocious. Although in Nottingham the attempt to destroy a mill was aborted before considerable damage had been done,[58] on other occasions, for instance in Norwich, rioters were far more successful in targeting producers' property:

> 'The new mill (a very large and expensive building) is almost entirely down, the flour sack after sack, thrown into the river, and the Proprietors books, receipts, and some money, all stolen or destroyed. At night every baker in town had his windows broke, and many had their furniture demolished in

54 *Journal*; 4th October 1766; p. 3.
55 *Journal*; 18th October 1766; p. 1.
56 *Journal*; 4th October 1766; p. 1.
57 Thompson; p. 71-2.
58 *Journal*; 11th October 1766; p. 3.

the streets. [...] A large malt house is now actually in flames, several houses [torn] down [...].'[59]

The account of flour being spoiled shows that the destruction of property could even take priority over procuring provisions.

The *Journal's* report of the riots in Bradford and Trowbridge recounts other attacks on traders' property when crowds were 'not only showing their resentment to the dealers in corn and flour [as well as] cheese and other provisions' by smashing up and expropriating property, but also by 'laying them under injunctions not to deal in those articles [in] the future.'[60]

Rioters often acted in an organised and coordinated way, for example recorded in the accounts of rioters systematically searching the traffic going in and out of Leicester. This could also be the case in attacks on property, such as in the riot in Gloucester where rioters organised themselves in small groups and targeted a number of houses where they were 'extorting money or taking away whatever they thought proper'. There rioters coordinated their actions using horn signals and calling for reinforcements when they met resistance, apparently causing significant damage:

> '[...] some [traders in provisions] have had their houses pulled down to the ground, their furniture broke to pieces, and the bedding cut to-bits; some have had nothing left but the clothes on their backs'.[61]

Threats were also directed against the property of local officials, for example in Norwich where an anonymous letter was:

> '[...] sent to our worthy Mayor, threatening to lay his house in ashes if he don't immediately regulate the price of flour, and set the rioters under confinement at liberty.'[62]

3.5. Clashes with constables, soldiers, gentlemen '&c.'

Although any attempt to categorise the severity of the riots is difficult and to an extent arbitrary, roughly half of the accounts of Food Riots reported on significant clashes, substantial attacks on property (other than the expropriations of provisions), the deployment of soldiers and/or on fatalities. The latter two factors, each reported in about a fifth of the riots, did not necessarily correlate with each other. A number of persons were not killed by the military, but by other, often self-appointed, civilian law enforcers.[63]

---

59 *Journal*; 4th October 1766; p. 3.
60 Ibid.; p. 4.
61 *Journal*; 25th October 1766; p. 3.
62 Ibid.; p. 4.
63 See *Journal*; 4th/11th/18th/25th October; 1st November 1766.

During the Food Riot in Gloucester one rioter was shot 'at a shopkeeper's' house, possibly whilst trying to expropriate goods. This 'so enraged the rest' of the rioters that the shopkeeper's house was destroyed whilst the shooter, 'by favour of the night, escaped [and] for fear of their vengeance, will not dare to return [to] his family'. In the aftermath of the riot, the local authorities were pressured to prosecute the shopkeeper:

> 'The mobs obliged the coroner and his jury to bring in the shopkeeper guilty of wilful murder otherwise they threatened to murder them, threatening vengeance to them and all others who would not comply with their unjust demands.'[64]

Whereas it is likely that this death was not the result of organised but spontaneous resistance to the rioters, on a number of occasions local officials called upon unofficial law enforcers to quell riots when there were neither adequate numbers of constables nor military forces available. This occurred for instance in Norwich, where the 'court [...] summoned every house keeper to take a staff and oppose the rioters.'[65]

On a number of occasions not only the rioters, but also their opponents organised themselves. This apparently was the case in Chippenham, where during a Food Riot 'the gentlemen [...] interposed, took possession of the mill, and bidding [the rioters] defiance, saved it from destruction.'[66] Another example is the case of a riot in Somerset which escalated into a full scale battle:

> '[A] large mob of poor people, consisting of near 2,000, went to North Bradley mill, and pulled down part of it [...]. From whence they set out for Beekington mill, [where they] were met by [...] Thomas Prowse [MP] and several other gentlemen [who] laid before them the dangerous consequences of such proceedings, desiring them to disperse, and assured them of his best endeavours for their relief. To this they replied, they had not eaten a morsel of bread for three days, but had subsisted on grains, &c, and that their wives and families were in the same miserable condition. They then resolutely proceeded forward to the mill. The miller, having assistance and fire-arms, discharged them among the mob. On this a battle ensured, in which many of the rioters were wounded; one is since dead; and 'tis said others cannot recover. Their ammunition being expended, the mob set fire to a faggot pile,

64 *Journal*; 25th October 1766; p. 3.
65 *Journal*; 4th October 1766; p. 3: The report did not contain information about the outcome of that confrontation.
66 *Journal*; 11th October 1766; p. 3.

> a mow of hay of twelve tons, a stable, the dwelling house and mill. The people within narrowly escaped their fury.'[67]

An astounding Food Riot on the border of Derbyshire and Leicestershire is not only another example of self-organisation on both sides but is also interesting as local officials repeatedly refused to become involved in what soon became serious fighting. After having received 'intelligence' of a sizeable stash of cheese being lodged in a warehouse adjacent to the river Trent, 'a mob of people not exceeding 100, principally women and children' expropriated allegedly as much as twenty hundredweights of cheese[68] before returning to their nearby village of Donington. As they were retreating, they were pursued by 'a person concerned in part of the property thus taken away' who had 'collected together a few men [...] taking from all they overtook what cheese they were loaded with and nine of the rioters prisoners.' The prisoners had to be released after their captors failed to persuade Donington's Justice of the Peace to issue warrants 'either for want of sufficient informations, or perhaps, not chusing to meddle in the matter'.[69] The following day a rather ugly battle ensued as rioters returned to the warehouse:

> '[...] a mob, more formidable in numbers [...] were fir'd upon by a guard of about 18 men, planted in the warehouse purposely to defend it; notwithstanding the fire-arms the mob assaulted the warehouse with great fury; but the people within keeping a continual fire of grape and small shot, and being besides assisted by some flanking parties who fir'd whenever the back part of the warehouse was assaulted in about two hours they dispersed: About 4 o'clock in the morning, they return'd again, some of them with fire-arms, but the people within keeping a continual fire as before, about six o'clock they thought proper to retreat.[70]

Nothing is known about casualties on either side. The day after saw further fierce clashes, to which I will refer hereafter simply as the Battle of Donington. The 'owners of the cheese, joined by several farmers and others on horseback, about 30 in number, with a considerable number of footmen' decided to go to the offensive and marched towards the village 'in search of the rioters'. However, they failed again in gaining the cooperation of the Justice of the Peace who did not grant the 'General Search Warrants', 'rather [choosing] to avoid acting at all surrounded with a numerous mob, in a village distant from any assistance' which apparently greatly vexed the company:

---

67 *Journal*; 4th October 1766; p. 4: The fires could be extinguished after the rioters had retreated.

68 Ibid.

69 *Journal*; 11th October 1766; p. 3.

70 Ibid.

> '[...] it is said some menaces, and other ill language were used by some of the company, not altogether so respectful as might have been expected to a gentleman in the commission of the peace. Finding they could not procure the warrants, they [decided] to seize upon the most suspected persons, concern'd in the late riots, and carry them before some other magistrate; they [...] rode up to the justices house, and ('tis said, but we hope is not true) broke open his outer gates, struck at his doors and windows with great violence [...].'[71]

Apparently at this point 'the town's people were exasperated' and:

> '[...] joined the mob, who began the assault upon the cheese-factors and their attendants, by discharging a great number of brick bats, stones, &c. The horsemen being thus attacked in front and flank, the people shouting, and vollies of stones falling from the hills, (where the women and children were planted in rows five or six deep;) the horses became ungovernable, and falling back upon their footmen, a scene follow'd of inconceivable confusion; both horse and foot fled with the utmost precipitation, pursued by the victorious mob who followed them quite down to the bridge, where a faint attempt was made to replace the guard in the warehouse, but the panic was so great, that the men refus'd to stand to their arms, and the mob were suffer'd to enter without any molestation. One of the cheese-factors, in his fright, is said to have forc'd his horse into the river, and swam the Trent. [72]

In the wake of the attackers' hasty retreat, the warehouse was 'soon emptied [...] of about two ton of cheese'. Although most of the cheese had been removed earlier using two boats, both were seized and their cargo expropriated, the rioters rejecting the owner's offer of selling the cheese at reduced rates (see 3.1.).[73]

> 'The bells rang at Donington, as if a signal victory had been obtain'd, and a hogshead of ale is said to have been given to the populace.'[74]

On the following day further boats and warehouses were targeted and large amounts of cheese seized. The tide only changed with the arrival of

---

71 Ibid.

72 Ibid.

73 Ibid. See *Journal*; 18th October 1766; p. 3: Some of the cheese was later 'restor'd back to the owners' by 'the poor people', probably in support of those which were later arrested or to prevent further arrests.

74 *Journal*; 11th October 1766; p. 3.

cavalry troopers in the area, almost a week after the first expropriations had taken place. On the 9th October 30 to 40 persons were arrested as they attempted to empty another warehouse. However, this was not yet the end of the affair. The arrival of the prisoners in Derby incited yet another riot:

> '[The rioters] have been brought in a carriage [...] to our goal: which has greatly exasperated our mob, who insulted the Magistrates, till they were oblig'd to read the Riot Act; and the soldiers were now driving, with sword in hand, all such as have not dispersed: The officer who commanded 'em I am inform'd has been terribly wounded, by stones &c. thrown at him, and some of the soldiers, two of which are at my door, bleed shockingly. I have just been out, and find very few remaining, but am afraid we shall have a very dreadful night.'[75]

In the end rioting and expropriations in the vicinity were not quelled until further military contingents arrived. According to a commentator in Derby it would have been 'impossible to keep the mob in any bounds, but from the fear they show to the military power.'[76]

The *Journal's* reports account of the ferocity and determination with which people on both sides did fight in Food Riots. A full picture cannot be established from only this single source and it is very possible that the newspaper's editors and its informants may have spiced up this very dramatic story. It seems however convincing that, confronted with and feeling abandoned by the weakness of the official law enforcers, some of the local traders and producers of provisions decided to act themselves and that they were willing to kill in order to stop people obtaining cheese. It is also believable that, in the absence of any forces to enforce his orders or even to ensure his own safety, the local Justice of the Peace had decided not to act, which apparently led to the unusual situation that he was rescued by the crowds when they attacked the cheese-owners and their associates.

In these examples the weakness of the British regime and its inability to quell the riots without having to call on local gentlemen and their 'associates', for example farm labourers, is striking. But on many occasions only professional soldiers were able to effectively repress rioters and this repeatedly took some time as troops were spread rather thinly.[77]

---

75 Ibid.

76 Ibid.

77 See *Journal*; 4th October 1766; p. 3; 11th October 1766; p. 3: For some information regarding troop movements. See *Journal* 18th October 1766; p. 1: Apparently this was not only the case in the Midlands. There were reports from Oxford regarding 'the many applications from a great variety of places' on 'his Majesty's troops' which were 'now almost entirely disposed in, or as near as possible in the neighbourhood of the places chiefly infested with these disorders.'

The used *Journal* issues contain limited details regarding the riots during which soldiers were deployed. However, it is apparent that the deployment of soldiers did not automatically result in fatalities. A crucial factor determining the level of violence perpetrated by the military appears to have been the attitude of local officials. In the riot in Leicester a contingent of infantry was available and 'almost instantly upon the spot, and form'd into a square, with bayonets fix'd, and in about twenty minutes were join'd by the whole regiment, who form'd as they came up, and soon clear'd the street.' Despite this rather intimidating display of force the crowds did not disperse but 'continued assembling in greater numbers, and behav'd with great insolence'. However, the Magistrate was 'desirous if possible to restore peace without proceeding to extremities' and tried instead to 'appease the mob' by organising the sale of cheese at reduced rates.[78]

On other occasions military forces did act with the utmost brutality against rioters. The *Journal* reports on a massacre in Warwickshire which left eight persons dead after a riot broke out when prices soared following the export of grain to Bristol. No more details were reported but this riot stood out as it resulted by far in the greatest (reported) number of deaths.[79]

3.6. Arrests and liberation attempts

On a number of occasions rioters had successfully enforced price reductions or expropriated large quantities of provisions, often meeting only little or no resistance by official and unofficial law enforcers. The rioters' successes, as well as the sheer number of events and the ferocity of some riots did spark anxiety as 'Trade and Business cannot be carried on with safety'[80] and successful rioting in one area seemed to lead to similar action in nearby towns and villages.[81] Therefore, harsh repressive measures were ordered, for example in local quarter sessions:

> '[...] these disorders have rather increased than diminished, and [...] the mob [has] become daily more numerous and more insolent. [...] [Therefore it was] unanimously agreed [at the quarter sessions in Oxford] to use the most vigorous measures for suppressing all future outrages [...].'[82]

---

78 *Journal*; 4th October 1766; p. 3.

79 *Journal*; 18th October 1766; p. 1.

80 *Journal*; 11th October 1766; p. 4.

81 See e.g. *Journal*; 4th October; p. 3; 18th October; p. 1.

82 Ibid. See Emsley; pp. 13-4: 'Offenders were brought before one of three principal kinds [of courts] during the eighteenth and nineteenth centuries: petty sessions, quarter sessions or assizes. [...] The courts of quarter sessions heard more serious offences that were prosecuted on indictment. [...] The verdicts at quarter sessions were decided by juries but the magistrates decided upon the sentence.'

Official resolutions like this were mirrored by private statements, for example by a commentator from Gloucester, demanding prosecutions to discourage further disturbances as well as continued military presence:

> 'If some examples are not made of the ringleaders [...] in order to prevent these insurrections, no man's life or property can be secure [...].'[83]

Making examples of so called ringleaders required arrests, which were reported in about a third of the examined Food Riots. This repeatedly triggered very determined liberation attempts, not only in Nottingham and Derby but also in Birmingham and Leicester where 'Four women behaving with great insolence to the Magistrates were taken and committed to gaol'. One of the women was 'instantly' 'rescued from the Constables' before an attempt was made to liberate the others:[84]

> '[...] the mob assembled in great numbers at the gaol, determin'd to rescue the prisoners, and with brickbats and stones entirely destry'd every pane of glass fronting the streets; they also forced open the outer door of the gaol [...], from whence the prisoners had been just removed.'[85]

Unfortunately the crowds not only failed to liberate the prisoners, but five so called 'ringleaders' were arrested when the attack on the goal was eventually repelled. On the next day the gaol was guarded by up to a hundred soldiers, each issued with fifteen rounds and ordered to open fire on any crowd trying 'to rescue the prisoners'.[86]

Arrests repeatedly occurred after the actual riots had ended. At the quarter sessions in Oxford warrants were issued 'against upwards of thirty [...] who have committed outrages in that neighbourhood'.[87] Following the Battle of Donington and the aforementioned arrest of over thirty persons, seven more were arrested and brought to Derby.[88] A troop of Dragoons 'quartered in Gloucester, have had full employ' rounding up alleged rioters:

> 'The number now in that goal is upwards of 60; but those who have fled the country upon this occasion, we are told, exceed 400; many of whom have left wives and large families to be maintained by their parishes.'[89]

---

83 *Journal*; 25th October 1766; p. 3.

84 *Journal*; 4th October 1766; p. 4; 11th October 1766; p. 4.

85 *Journal*; 4th October 1766; p. 3.

86 Ibid.

87 *Journal*; 18th October 1766; p. 1.

88 Ibid.; p. 3.

89 *Journal*; 1st November 1766; p. 3. See *Journal*; 25th October 1766; p. 3: Apparently it was not unusual that suspected rioters fled their homes. After the rioting in Hinckley 'upwards of' eighty people were said to have disappeared.

On occasion, these arrests were resisted. After the quarter sessions in Leicestershire, warrants were issued to seize a number of persons deemed to having been ringleaders in a riot in Hinckley. After two persons had been apprehended, a large crowd not only refused to disperse when the riot act was read but 'forced themselves into the room where the prisoners were confin'd, and in open violation of all law and authority set them at liberty.' This resulted in a sizeable military operation involving 'a troop of dragoons' and militia who arrested a further four persons. This time there was no such determined liberation attempt although a few stones were hurled and a shot was taken at the jailor.[90]

From the examined *Journal* issues little is known of what happened to those who were arrested during or after the riots and were not liberated. Following the riots in Norwich 'twelve or more' were in custody, 'charged with capital offences'.[91] However, although sentences were brutal, not all of those who were prosecuted would have faced the scaffold. William Derby and Thomas Russ were 'ordered to be publickly whipped, and to give security for their good behaviour for six months, and to remain in goal till such security is given' by the general quarter sessions. That five others rioters 'were ordered to remain till the assizes'[92] might indicate that these were condemned to harsher punishments.

---

90 *Journal*; 4th October 1766; p. 4; 18th October 1766; p. 3. See *Journal*; 1st November 1766; p. 4: The names of 'Thomas Grimes, Sarah Bonner, John Langham, John Blower, John Grondridge, William Hawey, Abraham Pettiser And Thomas Langham, all of Hinkley. William Halford of Desford. Will. Bull and Tho. Bull of Burbage' were published who were charged with assembling in a: 'Riotous and Tumultous Manner, committing divers Outrages and Violences, [...] and forcing themselves into the Room, where the Constables had two Persons in Custody for Felony, and feloniously rescuing and setting them at Liberty. Notice is hereby Given, That if any Person will apprehend or give Notice [...], so that any of the Offenders may be brought to Justice, they shall be handsomly Rewarded. And all Persons are caution'd not to harbour or relive them, as they will be deemed Accessary to their Crimes.'

91 *Journal*; 18th October 1766; p. 4. See Field; p. 14: '"Guilty – Death," were familiar words in the criminal courts. It was death to steal mutton – death requited the industry of the burglar, the shoplifter, and the coiner – death attended all, and was regarded as the great conservator of social security. [...] The murderer feared little worse than the robber of a hen-roost. Thrust alike into an underground cell, they were led forth at the appointed hour, to expiate their crime on Gallows-hill.'

92 *Journal*; 25th October 1766; p. 1.

4. Preventative appeasement

Aside from reports of the riots themselves, the *Journal* printed a number of official proclamations and articles providing information on how the rioters' better off contemporaries, state and local officials as well as propertied private citizens, sought to prevent further unrest. In communicating such measures to a wider audience, media like the *Journal* may have played a vital role.[93]

4.1. Measures to cap prices

On a number of occasions rioters attempted to stop the export of provisions from their area. This implies that the real or presumed scarcity of provisions was perceived by many rioters as one of the primary reasons for the 'dearness of provisions'. Therefore the issue of international exports of wheat had the potential of further fuelling social tensions. According to the *Journal*, the 1766 Food Riots occurred in a year which saw considerable crop failures all over Europe. Notable exceptions included Spain and England, allegedly enabling exports of English wheat to 'foreign markets' at almost 'unlimited prices'.[94] Whether or not these could really have resulted in a situation where the 'Majesty's subjects would be in danger of want, whilst foreigners are supplied from this country', soaring prices and anxieties about an increase in popular unrest appear to have been very real, especially as the price of wheat was 'upon the strongest ground presum'd to be still rising'. As Parliament was not to sit before November, the king was urged in late September to stop the exports of wheat:

---

93 See *Journal*; 4th October; p. 3; 11th October 1766; p. 2. Without further information it is difficult to ascertain who this audience consisted of, but it is always possible to take a (more or less) educated guess. One repeatedly reprinted proclamation was entitled 'To the Rioters', warning them of the consequences of their actions. It is possible that this and similar proclamations were not so much directed at rioters themselves but rather at 'respectable' readers, reassuring them that the law enforcers were determined to prosecute any rioters. See *To the Castle!* ...; chapters 4.3.; *Journal*; 11th October 1766; p. 3; 25th October 1766; p. 1: However, given that political issues like export embargos were discussed in public houses it can be assumed that the practise of reading and debating newspapers to/with each other was well established in all social classes well before the nineteenth century, which might also indicate that quite a few rioters were aware of 'To the Rioters' and similar messages. See *Journal*; 11th October 1766; p. 2: Among further evidence that papers like the *Journal* were read by the rioters are messages like the one by the cheese trader from Sapcote, trying to reassure readers that he was not involved in the export of provisions.

94 *Journal*; 4th October 1766; pp. 1/4. See Beckett (a); pp. 31/64-5: Britain had been a net exporter of grain for quite some time, subsidised and promoted by the government to stop prices collapsing as production increased. However, the net surplus of wheat production had begun to 'even out' by the mid-1760s and even turned into deficits in the 1770s.

> '[His Majesty has] to stop the progress of a mischief daily encreasing, and which if not immediately provided against, might be productive of calamities past of possibility of remedy. It is therefore upon the grounds of the above urgent necessity now impending, and for the safety, benefit, and sustenance of his Majesty's subjects, that his Majesty, with the advice of his Privy-Council, doth order [...] That an Embargo be forthwith laid upon all ships and vessels, laden or to be laden [...] with Wheat or Wheat-Flour to be exported to foreign parts [...].'[95]

Exports had repeatedly been suspended 'in years of dearth' during the eighteenth century, for example in 1707, 1740 and 1757.[96] Also in 1766 an embargo was ordered, along with instructions to 'his Majesty's Customs' to enforce it. In Bristol, monetary incentives were promised to hasten the return of ships laden with wheat so that 'the poor about that city [could be] provided with bread.' It is however questionable how efficient such a temporary embargo was and whether it could be effectively enforced. Apparently it was quite common to simply stash large quantities of wheat aboard boats on rivers, anticipating that the embargo would be lifted by November. Another measure taken on a national level was the prohibition of 'the making, extracting or distilling, of any kind of Low-Wines, or Spirits, from any Wheat, Wheat Meal, Wheat Flour, or Wheat Barn, or any Mixture therewith'.[97]

Although the *Journal* did report that prices fell in a number of counties after the proclamation of these policies,[98] it is impossible to validate without further research whether prices did actually fall nor whether any such reductions would have been connected to the embargo or the prohibition of distilling. It seems more likely that both policies would have had psychological rather than economic effects. They also had the potential to backfire. The prohibition of distilling alcohol from wheat, in previous decades officially supported in order to stabilise wheat prices during times of growing output,[99] may have resulted in a price increase for alcohol which, as can be assumed with ample surety, would not have been very popular. Furthermore the embargo on wheat resulted in increased exports of other crops, which in turn was feared to result in 'wheat as well as every other kind of grain, [becoming] much dearer':

---

95 *Journal*; 4th October 1766; p. 1. See *Journal* 25th October 1766; p. 4: There were demands to pass legislation automatically triggering an embargo whenever a certain level of domestic prices of wheat would be exceeded.

96 Beckett (a); p. 31.

97 *Journal*; 4th October 1766; pp. 1/3-4; *Journal*; 1st November 1766; p. 1.

98 *Journal*; 4th October 1766; p. 4; 18th October 1766; p. 1.

99 Beckett (a); p. 31.

'[...] for, between the exporting factors and the distillers, every handful of beans, peas and barley, are bought up almost at any price that is asked for them which must add to the distress of the poor as well as greatly diminish the revenue arising from the duties on malt and beer.'[100]

Aside from these policies on a national level, local authorities tried to increase the quantities of wheat on offer in the local markets. In Loughborough a number of officials and 'principal gentlemen' gave 'all due Encouragement to their Tenants to Thrash their Grain of all kinds' and promised 'all possible protection' to 'their Persons and Properties' when transporting provisions to markets as well as promising to secure 'the peaceable sale of all Commodities that shall be brought to Market'.[101]

The *Journal* also repeatedly reported on attempts of preventative appeasement by charity, explicitly initiated to have 'the dersir'd effect' of keeping 'all things [...] perfectly quiet.' There are a number of references to gentlemen engaging in charitable collections and donations in order to 'relieve the truly necessitous'. In Leicester '20 gentlemen had subcrib'd together a fund [and] directed the money be laid out in cheese to be sold all winter at a low price for the benefit of the poor.' Similarly in Coventry an 'old farmer' made 'experimental proof' of relieving the poor and 'preserving peace, at this time of want and confusion [...] and it would be well for the public if all who can afford it would imitate him.' His plan was to sell beef, cheese and wheat at cheap rates, thereby proving 'how easy any town may be kept in peace, and the poor supplied with provisions; especially if the rich will but open their purses'.[102]

Such charitable efforts were commented on very positively in the *Journal*, one article stating that:

'[...] many of [the industrious poor] would starve [...], were it not that some worthy and public-spirited gentlemen [...] continue to have bread privately conveyed from this city and other distant places to the several villages, where it is distributed to the poor at the same price that is given for it.'[103]

The recurring attacks on the property of traders and producers of provisions indicate that many people thought these groups contributed to or at least profited from the high level of prices. In Thompson's words:

---

100 *Journal*; 18th October; p. 4.

101 *Journal*; 25th October 1766; p. 4.

102 *Journal*; 18th October 1766; p. 3; 1st November 1766; p. 1: Amusingly the 'old farmer's' plan was said to have really been a vile popish plot. The accused allegedly responded that 'those of C[oventry], who have so long been accustomed to do evil, [cannot] of sudden learn to do well, until some other towns have shamed them into it.'

103 *Journal*; 25th October 1766; p. 3.

> 'In the popular mind, [forestalling] encompassed any exploitative action calculated to raise the price of provisions, and in particular the activities of factors, millers, bakers, and all middlemen.[104]

Therefore, commentators and officials were busy blaming and taking action against 'all Forestallers, Engrossers and Regrators':[105]

> '[It is] being alleged that [the recent] Disturbances arise from the present high price of Provisions, and that certain Individuals by Forestalling, Ingrossing and Regrating of the Necessaries of Life, and selling them again at their own price add greatly to the present apparent Scarcity'.[106]

A number of proclamations stated the intent to prosecute and fine anyone engaged in such activities and demanded the denunciation of 'any Offender'. Local officials, for example in Leicester or Derby, implemented this following a royal proclamation to 'preserve the Peace of the County, and Redress as much as possible the Complaints, of the Poor'.

Imposing 'strict orders' to stop trading outside 'public markets' was another attempt to counteract forestalling. The *Journal* reported on and printed proclamations to that end, for instance from Warwick, where the 'Mayor, Recorder and Justices of this Borough' gave 'Public Notice' that all persons were required to 'produce their respective Provisions in open Market' at set times and that no 'Person will be allowed to purchase any Provisions till they have been produced in the open Market.'[107]

Although the *Journal* mentions cases of persons being prosecuted and fined for forestalling, for example eleven in Glasgow and fourteen in Leeds,[108] it is not possible to ascertain without further research to what extent people were prosecuted and whether this had any effect on the development of prices. Again it seems far more likely that the action against forestalling was designed to have a psychological effect rather than measurable economic consequences. Prosecutions of true or alleged forestallers were very popular among large parts of the general populace

---

104 Thompson; p. 72.

105 *Journal*; 17th October 1766; p. 3. See Walker; pp. 182/218/444: In this context all three terms mean essentially the same. One of the meanings of 'To Engross' is defined as: 'to purchase the whole of any commodity for the sake of selling at a high price.' 'Forestaller' is defined as: 'One that anticipates the market, one that purchases before others to raise the price.' The entry for 'To Regrate' refers the reader to the other two terms.

106 *Journal*; 11th October 1766; p. 4.

107 Ibid.; *Journal*; 18th October 1766; p. 3; 25th October 1766; p. 1; 1st November 1766; p. 3.

108 *Journal*; 25th October 1766; p. 1; 1st November 1766; p. 3.

and 'some Tory paternalists', for Thompson further evidence of prevailing notions of an 'old paternalist moral economy' (see chapter 6.). However, by the end of the century, most of the old legislation against forestalling had been 'repealed or abrogated.'[109]

4.2. Threats and blame

Aside from promoting attempts to cap prices, a number of proclamations printed in the *Journal* contain threats as to the consequences of rioting, thereby not only waving a carrot, but also a big stick at the rioters in order to discourage further direct action. These threats were two-fold: firstly regarding the personal consequences for those involved in direct action, and secondly claiming that the rioting would spoil any measures to relieve economic distress.

A rather typical proclamation by a number of local officials and gentlemen in Derby started by listing the measures taken in an attempt to cap prices, and stated their intention to prosecute all 'Forestallers, Engrossers and Regrators' to the 'utmost of their power'. The proclamation then states that all possible resources will be used 'to quell all riots'. Interestingly this proclamation also contains a threat aimed at 'all Constables and Persons charged to aid and assist them'. These were threatened with prosecution should they 'neglect their Duty'. This indicates that events in Donington, where the local Justice of the Peace had chosen not to interfere, was not an isolated case, but similar cases occurred regularly enough that it was deemed necessary to threaten repercussions to anyone neglecting their 'duty'.[110]

A report from Newbury on charitable efforts to supply the 'industrious poor' with affordable bread was also ended with the threat that, should a 'tumultuous assembly' of 'any disorderly persons' gather, the riot act would be read immediately.[111]

Elsewhere people were assured that, whilst anything was being done to relive the plight of the 'truly necessitous':

> '[...] the powers of government will upon all occasions be exerted with the utmost vigour and force against every individual who shall dare to insult the execution of law and

---

109 Thompson; pp. 72-3.

110 *Journal*; 18th October 1766; p. 3.

111 *Journal*; 4th October 1766; p. 4. See *Journal*; 11th October 1766; p. 4; 25th October; p. 2: The relevant passages of the Riot Act were repeatedly printed in the *Journal*: 'Our Sovereign Lord the King, Chargeth and Commandeth, all Persons being Assembled, immediately to Disperse themselves, and peaceably to depart to their Habitations, to their lawful Business, upon the Pains in the Act made in the First Year of King George the First, for preventing Tumults and Riotous Assemblies.'

> justice, or by unlawful [assembly] disturb the peace of that society of which they themselves are a part.'[112]

The proclamations contained not only threats to rioters, but also blamed them for prolonging the price crisis, for instance by stating that the 'people alone must take blame upon themselves, if they prevent the salutary measures taken for their relief answering the purpos'd intention.'[113] Frequently reprinted was a proclamation entitled 'To the rioters':

> 'The Consequences of your late Riots are Terrible: Thousands of you have been guilty of Felony; many already imprison'd, the Magistrates will do their Duty; what must be the Event to yourselves; without this necessary exertion of their Power you'll be all Starv'd; Think before [it is] too late. Every Thing that can be thought of has been done for your Benefit. The Exportation of Wheat is at an End; the Distillery is stopp'd; the Laws against Regrating and Forestalling are order'd to be put in Execution; Farmers have been requir'd to bring Provisions to Market. And nothing but your own Indiscretion can prevent your reaping the Benefit.'[114]

Rioters were also blamed for causing the problems in the first place, for 'introducing that very scarcity they pretend to remedy',[115] and said to:

> '[...] commit all sorts of enormities, which must occasion, where-ever these riots are, a local scarcity; and consequently make provisions dearer.[116]

Rather than obstructing 'the common channels of Justice',[117] people were urged to stay put, to rely on and trust in charitable gentlemen and policymakers, as well as repaying their wise leadership and generous

---

112 *Journal*; 18th October 1766; p. 3. See *Journal*; 11th October 1766; p. 4; 25th October; p. 2: One repeatedly reprinted proclamation threatened that anyone attempting to stop the Riot Act being read, not to disperse after it had been read, or attempting to 'Demolish or pull Down' any building 'shall be guilty of Felony without Benefit of Clergy'. Apparently the passage 'without the Benefit of the Clergy' means in this context that e.g. first-time offenders could not expect any lenience from the courts.

113 *Journal*; 18th October 1766; p. 3.

114 *Journal*; 4th October 1766; p. 3.

115 *Journal*; 25th October 1766; p. 1.

116 Ibid.; p. 4. See ibid.; p. 3: There is some evidence in the examined *Journal* issues to support such claims, e.g. in the report on the Gloucester Food Riot which stated that because the 'land here being chiefly in pasture, [it] raises not corn enough for its people; it depends on the neighbouring county for a support, which [is] now being retarded by these riotous proceedings'.

117 *Journal*; 25th October 1766; p. 1.

support of the truly needy with their collaboration in preventing riots and persecuting rioters. This was very elegantly communicated in a message to 'the Industrious Poor' of Leicester:

> 'You cannot but conceive that the better sort of People in this place have some feeling for your Distress. We have always our Hearts as well as Purses open for your Relief. Whenever the Times require it. You've had many Instances to convince you of this Truth. There are many amongst you who conceal their Grievances, who are proper objects of our Benevolence; it is such as you that we Address. We have raised a capital Sum and purchased a quantity of Cheese to supply you during the winter season at a moderate price, and it will be disposed of to those Families at a low rate. All that is desired or expected from you, is a grateful return for the Care and Esteem we have of you. That you'll use your best endeavours to prevent Riots, and if possible to discover the Rioters, that they may be brought to justice. They are the bane of Society; the destruction of Property: and injurious to yourselves: none would be concerned in it but the Saucy and idle Poor, who wou'd live without labour. Of such as these severe Examples must be made; they must be cut off as proper Warnings to this and the next Generation.'[118]

[118] *Journal*; 18th October 1766; p. 3.

5. The depiction and identities of the rioters

Although the *Journal* articles contain many colourful descriptions of the rioters, there is little concrete evidence regarding their identities. A number of persons arrested for their alleged involvement in the riots were named, but the used sources do not provide any further information about them. Therefore the only information which can be derived from the names is the gender of these persons. All but one of the named rioters appear to have been male, a ratio which is surprising considering the recurring accounts of women rioters. Women were frequently mentioned in the reports of the riots, being described to have been involved in expropriations, stopping exports and irritating as well as actively fighting law enforcers. Women also became targets of repression, being arrested during riots and in their aftermath.[119]

The fact that women did play a significant role in all aspects of Food Riots is hardly surprising as women were always involved in organising and fighting social struggles. Astounding is the very fact that women's involvement in Food Riots is so explicitly mentioned. This can be interpreted as an attempt to reaffirm women's confinement to the domestic sphere. Joan O'Brien criticised historians who were/are downplaying or altogether ignoring women's involvement in all struggles but Food Riots, thinking it 'acceptable for women to act over food prices because this accords with the idea that they are, and always have been, domestic centred'.[120]

Assuming that this argument is also valid for the rioting women's contemporaries,[121] it appears the latter also tried to re-embed the perceived anomaly of rioting women in the gender regime by reporting it on those occasions when the women's direct action was related to the reproductive sphere.

Focussing on the activities of women rioters may also have been motivated by the attempt to systematically depict the rioters as being the antithesis of masculinity or 'Manishness', i.e. 'male [...] behaviour'.[122]

---

119 *Journal*; 4th October 1766; pp. 3/4; 25th October 1766; pp. 1/3; *Journal*; 1st November 1766; p. 4: After arrests in Gloucester the number of male and female prisoners was stated to have been 'seven men and six women'.

120 O'Brien; pp. 4/8-10.

121 See *To the Castle!* ...; chapters 1.1./4.2.: Although O'Brien's argument referred to historiography, it appears to be just as valid for the women rioters' contemporaries. Our research has highlighted that women's involvement in the 1831 Reform Riots was largely ignored, not only by historians but also by contemporary commentators of the riots, e.g. newspaper editors.

122 Worcester; column MAS.

The dominant concept of masculinity at the time appears to have been constructed around the concept of rationality. A dictionary from 1835 defines some trademarks of a man as him being an 'Individual [...] Not a beast' stating that when 'a person is out of his senses, we say, he is not his own man.' In this source manliness was primarily defined by what it is not (supposed to be), also describing it as behaviour that was not 'womanish' and not 'childish'.[123] Therefore a man was not supposed to act according to what was constructed as 'womanish', i.e. being a 'gentle, domestic brute'.[124]

When Wollstonecraft first published these often quoted words in 1792, the term 'brute' had various connotations aside the predominant modern understanding of simply describing a 'brutal person':

> 'Brute [...] Senseless. [...] Savage. [...] Bestial. [...] Rough; ferocious [...] An irrational creature; a savage.'[125]

Whereas a man was supposed to be in control of his senses, irrationality appears to have been at the core of one predominant concept of femininity. According to this, a woman would have never stopped being perceived as a 'brute', also defined in a dictionary from 1768 as a 'creature without reason'.[126] Even when a woman was engaged in rioting, thereby ceasing to be 'gentle', although not necessarily ceasing to be 'domestic' (see above), she did not cease to be perceived as a 'brute', becoming a 'ferocious' rather than a 'gentle' 'brute'. Therefore in the eyes of many of her contemporaries a woman would have been perceived as being unable to shed the trait of irrationality.

Adding to this picture in which rioting was apparently equated with irrationality is another striking pattern in the depiction of women rioters. They are repeatedly described as acting alongside children, for example when a crowd was described as 'principally [consisting of] women and children', or when provisions were being 'chiefly carried off by women and boys.' Also the report of the Battle of Donington mentions 'women and children' fighting side by side.[127] The constructs of childish and womanish behaviour and characteristics are similar. Wollstonecraft reflects on the idea of women's intellects being depicted as childlike[128] and in the aforementioned dictionary from 1768 'childish' was, among others things, also defined as 'ignorant'.[129]

According to this, both women and children engaging in direct action during Food Riots were directly and indirectly perceived and depicted as

---

123 Ibid.; column MAN.
124 Wollstonecraft; p. 29.
125 Worcester; column BUB.
126 Johnson; column BRY.
127 *Journal*; 4th October 1766; p. 3; 11th October 1766; p. 3.
128 Wollstonecraft; p. 29.
129 Johnson; column CHI.

being 'out of their senses', irrational 'brutes'. Descriptions of the male rioters, characterise them as 'desolate, idle fellows, that delight more in drinking than work', etc., being 'led on by ignorance and madness',[130] i.e. behaving out of their senses. Therefore it appears that all rioters, men, women and children, were constructed as being/behaving unmanly in the aforementioned sense, the former by choice, the latter were simply seen as having no choice, their behaviour, although perceived to be anomalous, still determined by and consistent with their age and/or gender. It appears that this depiction would have delegitimized as well as explained the rioters' actions for many readers of the *Journal*.

The descriptions of rioters offer more information about those describing than those described, but there are some scattered hints to rioters' occupations and levels of prosperity or poverty. In the Food Riot in Scarborough it was reported that the rioters were 'fishermen, fisherwomen, &c.'[131] indicating that those rioters were in employment, though in a trade which was subject to seasonal changes and probably did not offer the prospect of prosperity. Whereas one article mentions a 'large mob of poor people',[132] another one, reporting on a Food Riot in Gloucester, states that the rioters were not the 'very poorest of the people, who can earn but seven, eight, or nine shillings a week'. These 'poorest' persons are reported to have 'in general behaved soberly, and kept themselves industriously to their several callings.' The majority of rioters in this region were described as:

> '[...] sturdy young fellows, chiefly weavers, scribblers, and shearers, and could have earned from nine to near thirty shillings a week, as several of the gentlemen, their employers, have declared if they would have kept to their work.[133]

These claims have to be treated with the utmost care, not least because this description of the rioters ties in very neatly with the claim of drunkards being more interested in the price of booze than whether they can afford bare necessities like bread.

However, it is quite possible that workers with very small incomes played only a minor role in the riot in Gloucester and elsewhere, with better paid workers often taking the lead, simply because for those on minimal incomes

---

130 *Journal*; 25th October 1766; pp. 1/3.

131 Ibid.; p. 1.

132 *Journal*; 4th October 1766; p. 3.

133 *Journal*; 25th October 1766; p. 3. See ibid.; p. 4: 'the rioters will be found to consist not of the industrious poor with large families, but are made up of the idle [...]'. See Rudé; pp. 137-8: He identified 'wage earners, craftsmen, and small tradesmen' as taking a lead in Food Riots where they enforced 'a rough and ready kind of natural justice by breaking windows, burning their enemies of the moment in effigy, or 'pulling down' their dwelling-houses, pubs, or mills.'

losing a day's pay may have meant the difference between just about getting by and facing starvation. However, where people were without any means of survival at all, it appears that they did become actively involved in Food Riots, for example in Somerset where rioters were reported not to have eaten a 'morsel in three days'.[134]

134 *Journal*; 4th October 1766; p. 4.

6. (Silly) explanations for rioting and price developments

Depicting and debating the development of prices in general and short term fluctuations in particular is a complex and imprecise undertaking.[135] However, some of these difficulties derive from, as well as hint towards, an important aspect of the development of prices: even in a situation like in autumn 1766, where the majority of the accounts printed in the *Journal* indicate soaring prices, the picture is rather varied, with prices fluctuating significantly, not only over time but also in different regions. In a report from Lancaster the price of cheese was not only described as 'reasonable', but as cheaper than 'it has been for several preceding years'. However, a report from London stated the price of wheat had almost doubled,[136] compared to the 'general rate' in the year 1750.[137]

Whereas this evidence can at best be described as fragmentary, the numerous accounts of high prices from various regions, together with the occurrence of the riots themselves, demonstrate that in many areas food prices were perceived to significantly exceed 'customary' rates. To determine how this fits in with the overall development of prices in the mid-1760s would require further (and rather dull) research. However, this is (thankfully) not necessary to investigate the principal research questions.

Far more interesting are a number of articles printed in the *Journal* issues that debate reasons for price rises and the outbreak of riots, though some of them are primarily entertaining. One of the latter examples was printed in the *Journal's* first October issue and is a strange but most alarming tale contributed by 'a gentlemen in Paris' who exposes high prices to be the consequence of a devilish French plot. Although being utter nonsense, this report is well worth to be quoted at length:

---

135 See Rich/Wilson (a); pp. 374-8: They provide an introduction regarding various methodological challenges in analysing the development of prices. See Rich/Wilson (b); pp. 57-104 for a shedload of data regarding the European developments in agrarian output over c.300 years (1500-1800). See Beckett (a); p. 54 for a very brief description of developments in agricultural output in England. See Rich/Wilson (a); pp. 391-407/464/470/478/482-3 for figures regarding trends in the development of prices. Although these provide invaluable information about long term developments, it has to be remembered that they are mathematical abstractions of massive amounts of raw data, which are themselves based on various sources documenting and often simplifying highly complex social relations. Therefore these figures do at best not necessarily reflect the individual experiences of people living through these periods and will often contradict them.

136 *Journal*; 4th October 1766; p. 1; 1st November 1766; p. 1.

137 Field; p. 10.

> 'I find this court is very intent of putting two plans into execution, calculated for depopulating and starving the industrious poor of Great Britain, on one hand, and on the other, for making a plentiful provisions for, and multiplying the inhabitants of this already populous country; to effect both [...] it has been resolved to grant the vast forests and wastes in this kingdom to such foreigners as shall chose to cultivate them; and, at the same time to buy up corn enough in Great Britain for their support, which, they imagine, will create such a dearth there as must force the inhabitants to leave it; in consequence of which, they think numbers of them will chose to follow their native food to France, rather than take a long hazardous voyage to cultivate the inhospitable wilds of North America [...]. But [...] preventing the exportation of corn will be a great means of ruining this politic scheme [...].'[138]

Luckily these most cunning and devious plans were foiled by the wise king and Privy Council when they prohibited exports, thereby saving Britain once again from the vile French.

Less amusing but far more interesting is an article from October's final *Journal* issue. Its unknown author is trying to 'discover the cause' of the 'general distress' without 'pretend[ing] to know the antidote.' Although it needs to be criticised, the article is striking for its unusual level of reflection regarding the wider political and socioeconomic context of the events.[139]

The article discusses and criticises the focus on the issue of exports as well as the 'outcry [...] loudly raised against forestallers and regrators'. Although stating that the latter were a 'very bad sort of people', the author asks whether it is 'possible, is it probable, that their influence can extend to articles of general consumption, uniformly through all the markets in the nation', concluding that 'the evil lies deeper than this; and hunting these persons out is at best, but a wild goose chase'. Regarding the issue of wheat exportation it is argued that the very fact of the exports demonstrates that England was 'better provided than our neighbours', whilst the 'continuance of our complaints' is taken as an indication 'that the high price of the necessaries of life springs from a deeper source still.'[140]

Instead, the author identifies two policies which triggered the 'malady', namely the rise of duties and taxes 'which not only distress us at home, but must ruin us at foreign markets'. These were allegedly caused by the level of the national debt which rocketed during the recent Seven Years' War, this 'dance in Germany' by 'which we were to conquer America'. However, the

---

138 *Journal*; 4th October 1766; p. 4.

139 *Journal*; 25th October 1766; p. 3. See ibid.; p. 4: Another article gave very different explanations for price developments, arguing along Malthusian lines.

140 *Journal* 25th October 1766; p. 3.

author identifies the 'deeper source' of the price developments in the transformations taking place in the agricultural sector. The author's critique focuses on great landowners, living in 'greater luxury and profusion' than ever before 'in so expensive a place as London'. Tenants' rents were said to have been constantly raised, resulting in small tenancies being replaced by 'as large farms as tenants can be found to engage in':

> 'By this means a quantity of land [...] on which by careful cultivation [...] many industrious families might subsist in a decent independence, is engrossed by a wholesale undertaker, under whom those individuals who would form such families, are forced to work as servants.'[141]

The disappearance of small tenancies was also supposed to lead to the depopulation of rural areas, resulting in an increasing number of persons taking up trades outside the agricultural sector:

> '[...] there springs up a greater number of artisans than is proportionate to the quantity of commodities to be wrought; and a greater number of traders than the quantity of goods to be transferred will maintain.'[142]

The author assumed that both depopulation and urbanisation would have fatal consequences for the development of prices:

> 'The fewer hands any commodity is in, the more is the price of that commodity in their power. We have seen that land is held in large quantities and in few hands, which necessarily renders the produce of the land dear at the first hand; and the competition of the numbers which throng into every branch of manufactures, tends to reduce the price of labour, and lessen the profits of the articles wrought and dealt in; so that at the same time that the prices of goods are extravagantly raised, the artisan and trader can scarcely live.'[143]

The article finishes with a rather gloomy outlook on the consequences of these developments:

> '[...] property is seized by their creditors, and their business goes to their more successful neighbours. For as considerable dealers can afford to sell for less profit than their poorer neighbours, they therefore undersell them until they break them, when they swallow up their trade. Thus does a monopoly of land necessarily lead to a monopoly of trade; and

---

141 Ibid.
142 Ibid.
143 Ibid.

both to a general poverty, and a slavish dependence of the many on the few.'[144]

This article is an astounding analysis of the events in 1766. The author demonstrated rather elegantly that the popular obsession with 'evil' forestallers was a folly. Rather than focusing on the trading practices of 'evil' individuals or short term economic policies, the author examined changing production and property relations. However, by failing to explain the defining structure of English agrarian capitalism, 'landlord – capitalist tenant – wage labourer',[145] and ignoring the self-perpetuating development of the productive forces as a consequence of the primitive accumulation,[146] the author simply identifies the greed of the landlords to be at the root of the problems, failing to criticise the underlying social relations. The error of focussing on 'evil' forestallers is thereby repeated, although this time it is the landlords which are depicted as 'evil'.

The author's utopia, a society of semi-subsistent farmers living merrily on less greedy landowners' lands is not only reactionary in the very sense of the word, but also flawed as this was contradicted by the predominant mode of production. It ignores that the post-feudal form of surplus extraction in form of tenants' rents rather than peasants' labour initiated a process whereby farmers either became capitalist tenants or landless labourers. Though the emerging agrarian class structure was the result of persons' interactions and could therefore have been changed, any viable critique would need to go beyond blaming the actions and behaviour of specific individuals. Despite these and other errors of the unknown author, such as the denial of the massive increase in productivity which accompanied the changes in agriculture,[147] the article is not only a most interesting example for the continuities in the debates on agricultural transformations.[148] It also debates a number of developments in a surprisingly far-sighted manner, such the massive increase of workers in the textile industries, which were to result in atrocious living and working conditions, especially for nineteenth century framework knitters.[149]

---

144 Ibid.

145 Brenner; p. 63.

146 See Marx; pp. 659-707.

147 See Brenner; pp. 31/61-75: '[...] most significant for English agricultural development was the particularly productive use of the agricultural surplus promoted by the special character of its rural class relations; in particular, [...] by an emergent landlord-tenant symbiosis which brought mutual co-operation in investment and improvement.'

148 See Halhead: This mid-seventeenth century critique of agricultural transformation is not only a brilliant read but also shows that the majority of the arguments stressed by the unknown *Journal* author had been around for a very long time.

149 See *To the Castle!* ...; chapters 1.3./1.4.

Aside from the reasons for price developments, the outbreak of the riots and the motivation of rioters were debated in a number of *Journal* articles. The assumption that rioters acted 'on account of the dearness of provisions' was frequently rejected. A number of articles in the *Journal* issues state that the riots occurred only 'under pretence of distress from the high price of wheat, and other provisions' whereas it is instead 'well known, from their whole conduct, that [the rioters'] desire hath been more for liquor and plunder, than to redress grievances'.[150] However, judging 'from their whole conduct' the accusation that the rioters were embarking on a plundering rampage can be dismissed with ample surety. Although expropriations were the most common form of direct action during the riots, the rioters mostly expropriated basic foodstuffs. People seizing other goods or money is rarely mentioned.

One of the *Journal* articles explains the riots by recounting the common tale of the mysterious stranger stirring up trouble:

> 'The principal ringleader of all these riots is a stranger in this country; [...] he is said to have been bred a Lawyer and tells the people they have an authority to commit outrages of this kind, under pretence that the goods they take away have been Engrossed, and are forfeited by Law, which he pretends to justify by some fallacious Arguments drawn from the Kings-proclamation. This fellow is not yet taken.'[151]

Despite the ludicrousness of the tale of a vile stranger roaming the Midlands and giving legal lectures, the actions of the rioters do indeed indicate that many thought their actions justified, correcting price levels perceived to be immoral and not customary. Thompson described Food Riots as being:

> '[...] legitimized by the assumptions of an older moral economy, which taught the immorality of any unfair method of forcing up the price of provisions by profiteering upon the necessities of the people.'[152]

Reports like the one of the 'old woman', unimpressed by what she thought to be an 'extraordinary' price for butter, or of those persons declaring themselves 'regulators', back up this argument, as do the reports of punitive direct action against 'forestalling' traders and producers. For Thompson the latter indicated that a 'consumer-consciousness preceded other forms of political or industrial antagonism' and that in these early days of the

---

150 *Journal* 18th October 1766; p. 1; 25th October 1766; p. 3/4.

151 *Journal* 18th October 1766; p. 3.

152 Thompson; pp. 67-8. See ibid.; p. 73: '[...] behind every such form of popular direct action some legitimizing notion of right is to be found.'

Industrial Revolutions 'not wages, but the cost of bread, was the most sensitive indicator of popular discontent.'[153]

Thompson refers to examples of broad opposition against repressive measures to support his argument of Food Riots being widely perceived as 'acts of justice'.[154] Indeed, accounts like the report on the Battle of Donington, when apparently a whole village rose up, or when in the aftermath of these events inhabitants of Derby rioted as prisoners arrived at the town's goal, clearly demonstrate people's readiness to engage in very practical acts of solidarity with Food Rioters.

The rioters' reported 'conduct' strongly indicates that their primary aims were the procurement of provisions, correcting what was deemed not customary[155] and punishing those perceived to cause, worsen or profit from the high prices. It appears unlikely that the majority of rioters did have a wider political or economic agenda. The riots of autumn 1766 therefore appear to have been 'direct action on [a] particular grievance' but they did not develop into one of 'the great political risings of the "mob"'.[156]

The Food Riot, at least in the form debated in this book, appears to have been a specific phenomenon of popular protest in the early Industrial Revolution. Both Thompson and Rudé state that it 'did not long survive the arrival of the new industrial age'. Although it had been the 'prevailing form' of popular protest in the eighteenth and well into the nineteenth centuries,[157] and Food Riots were still occasional occurrences in the 1850s,[158] they soon became far less frequent events:[159]

> 'With the growth of urban population and the dawn of the factory system at the end of the century, trade unions became more frequent and more stable, and direct conflicts between wage-earners and employers a more common feature of industrial and urban communities. From the 1780's onwards strikes were beginning to eclipse food riots [...].'[160]

---

153 Ibid.; p. 68.

154 Ibid.; p. 70.

155 See Rudé; p. 237: He describes this rather more dramatically as 'natural justice'.

156 Thompson; pp. 66-7: He lists a number of examples where this did happen, e.g. the Gordon Riots of 1780 or the mobbing of the king in the streets of London in 1795 and 1820.

157 Rudé; p. 237; Thompson; p. 67.

158 See Field; p. 491; Beckett (b); p. 289.

159 Rudé; pp. 237-8.

160 Ibid.; p. 238.

Conclusions

> *'In considering [this] form of 'mob' action we have come upon unsuspected complexities [...]'.*[161]

The Great Cheese Riot has indeed proven to be more than just an entertaining footnote in Nottingham's turbulent history of social struggles. It was one event in a series of riots triggered by similar grievances and in which recurring patterns of rioters' direct actions and their opponents' reactions were clearly identifiable, as were patterns in the depiction of the rioters and their motives. The Food Riots were an example of a specific form of 'collective bargaining by riot'[162] in a time of fundamental socioeconomic transformation, bargaining by riot that was focussed on the market places of villages, towns and cities, and which did not yet focus on wages but on prices.

Examining these riots, a number of recurring patterns in the rioters' direct action could be identified. Examples were found for the direct enforcement of price reductions, a phenomenon that prominently featured in Thompson's depiction of Food Riots, though it seems crucial not to overestimate the importance of such events, as they were only reported on a few occasions.[163] In the majority of examples where prices were directly or indirectly reduced, the bargaining by riot (or by the threat of riot) resulted in a compromise. For the rioters' opponents this usually meant a swift end to the disturbances. But at least in the examples reported in the *Journal*, these events were also successes for the rioters who could rectify their immediate grievances without suffering casualties and whilst managing to avoid (or to reverse) arrests. Although the status quo prevailed when prices were temporarily renegotiated by direct action, in the examined cases all the rioters went home alive.

However, expropriations of goods were by far the most common feature in our sample of Food Riots, indicating that, on most occasions, rioters were not so much bothering with regulating prices to re-establish local customary terms of trade, but rather taking what they could, often demonstrating considerable levels of coordination and organisation in the course of their actions.

The perception of the price rises being caused by scarcity, triggered or worsened by 'evil' forestallers and producers motivated the attacks on property as well as the attempts to stop the removal of provisions from the

---

161 Thompson; p. 73.

162 Hobsbawm (a); p. 59.

163 See Thompson; p. 70: In other Food Riots this did happen in Nottingham as well, such as in 1795 when women 'went from one baker's shop to another, set their own price on the stock therein, and putting down the money, took it away.'

rioters' neighbourhoods. The tendency to focus on individual 'evil' persons rather than social relations also influenced the measures of preventative appeasement taken at local and national levels.

With regards to the attempts to quell the riots, a number of aspects are notable, prominently the fact that not only the rioters but also their opponents organised themselves, the latter repeatedly doing so as there simply were only few or no official law enforcers around.

As to the measures of preventative appeasement, they appear to have had little or no effects other than psychological ones, with officials on local as well as national levels desperately trying to demonstrate decisive action in tackling people's grievances, whilst at the same time announcing harsh action against anyone who would not repay such wise leadership with patient endurance. What can be assumed to have had actual effects were the actions of local propertied persons subsidising prices. This appears to have been the most effective measure taken to prevent further riots, especially as the capabilities of the British state to forcibly repress the riots appear to have been severely limited.

That it was possible to end and avert Food Riots by subsidising prices makes it quite clear that these events in autumn 1766 were no insurrectionist or revolutionary movement, but simply direct action taken by desperate people, caused by the particular grievance of soaring food prices. The majority of the rioters apparently did not strive for more than to rectify that grievance and punish those perceived to be at its cause, i.e. producers demanding high prices and traders suspected of forestalling or exporting of provisions. Although the laws of the propertied were temporarily defied by the rioters' direct action, most poignantly during the episode when charitable compromise was rejected by rioters who preferred straightforward expropriation, the principles of the property and production relations were never endangered during the autumn of 1766.

Although the identity of the rioters remains very vague, their depiction by their contemporaries was highly informative. That rioting women were not ignored but their actions highlighted in the *Journal*, something that first struck me as an anomaly, actually reflected the gender regime of the time as those commentating on the riots in the *Journal* were not only trying to incorporate the existence of women rioters in their worldview, but also using women's direct action to delegitimise the rioters. The depiction of women engaged in rioting is a subject matter that calls for more detailed research.

In hindsight, Nottingham's Great Cheese Riot appears as little more than a prelude for struggles which were to come, be it Luddism, the Reform Riots, Chartism, the General Strike or the Miners' Strike (to name just a few). Nevertheless it is an intriguing story which on closer inspection offers a lot of insight into the development of social relations in industrialising Britain.

The long tradition of Food Riots also needs to be remembered for its failures, such as rioters punishing 'evil' individuals rather than tackling the wider context of their grievances. However, that is no reason for People's Histreh to stop upholding the brilliant symbol of a loaf on a stick.

In the end it has to be admitted that the deliberations in this text regarding this highly complex form of popular protest are very much insufficient. The 1766 Food Riots were rooted in the changing social relations of English[164] society during the early days of the Industrial Revolution, which are not even roughly outlined, let alone sufficiently debated. Referring to (i.e. pinching a catchy phrase from) a fascinating debate regarding economic development in late medieval and (very) early modern Europe, I have to admit that I merely described aspects of Food Riots, but my deliberations are in no way sufficient to explain them.[165]

Furthermore, I was unable to find an answer to one of the most vexing questions on this subject matter: what type of cheese was rolled down Wheeler Gate?

---

164 Rudé; pp. 235-6: It has to be stated that the discussed form of the Food Riot was specific to a particular period in the development of modern bourgeois-capitalist societies and not specific to a certain area or country. Rudé refers to similarities of Food Riots in England and France.

165 Brenner; p. 36.

Appendices

I. Weights and Money

The following has been taken from Macdonald; pp. 174-5. Of all the imperial measurements and denominations only those are mentioned that have been mentioned in this text.

	Imperial (lb.)	Metric (kg.)
1 ton	2,240	1,016.7
1 hundredweight (cwt.)	112	50.8
1 pound (lb.)	1	0.5

A bushel is 'a dry measure of volume containing 8 gallons'. Therefore (if I have done my maths correctly/understood this odd measurement) a container that can hold 36 litres of water could hold one bushel of e.g. grain.

	shillings (s)	pennies (d)	halfpence (½d)	farthings (¼d)
1 pound sterling (£1)	20	240	480	960

One Guinea was worth £1.1s.0d (one pound and one shilling or twenty-one shillings or 252 pence).

Prices were often written in formats such as e.g. £1.5s.8d (one pound, five shillings and 8 pence), or 6/3 (six shillings and three pence) or 4/- (four shillings).

II. Summary of the Food Riots

This is a summary of the examined sample of Food Riots. Please keep in mind that this table has been compiled on the basis of the information provided by the used sources. Therefore this is a summary of what was reported in the *Journal* and not of what actually happened.

The vast majority of Food Riots could only be dated indirectly, often based on phrases such as 'Saturday last'. Five could not be dated at all; although three of those were reported in the issue dated 4th October and the other two in the issue dated 18th October and must therefore have occurred prior to these dates. Another riot, reported in the issue dated 25th October could only be dated based on the rather vague description that it happened 'last week'.

The counties are stated according to modern county borders. Place names are stated in their modern forms.

Date(s)	**County/Counties & Places**	**price reductions (directly enforced)**	**price reductions (indirectly enforced)**	**(attempted) expropriations**	**(attempted) stopping of exports**	**attacks on property**	**clashes of rioters and law enforcers**	**military deployed**	**fatal injuries/ fatalities**	**arrests**	**(attempted) prisoner liberations**	**reported in Journal issue dated**	**Notes**
9th–11th Sep	Oxfordshire; Oxford		✓	✓	✓							4th Oct; p. 1	-
24th Sep	Worcestershire; Worcester											4th Oct; p. 4	details of direct action unknown
26th Sep	West Midlands; Coventry	✓			✓							4th Oct; p. 3	same rioters as in Nuneaton

Date(s)	27th Sep	27th-28th Sep	28th Sep	29th-30th Sep	30th Sep-2nd Oct	2nd-5th Oct
County/Counties & Places	Warwickshire; Nuneaton	Norfolk; Norwich	Buckinghamshire; Great Barlow	West Midlands; Birmingham	Leicestershire; Leicester	Nottinghamshire; Nottingham
price reductions (directly enforced)			✓			
price reductions (indirectly enforced)	✓			✓	✓	
(attempted) expropriations		✓	✓		✓	✓
(attempted) stopping of exports					✓	✓
attacks on property		✓				✓
clashes of rioters and law enforcers		✓	✓		✓	✓
military deployed					✓	✓
fatal injuries/ fatalities						1
arrests			7-8	✓	9	2-3
(attempted) prisoner liberations				✓	✓	✓
reported in Journal issue dated	4th Oct; p. 3	4th Oct; p. 3	18th Oct; p. 4	11th Oct; p. 4	4th Oct; p. 3	11th Oct; p. 3
Notes	same rioters as in Coventry	-	-	number of those arrested not stated	-	Great Cheese Riot

Date(s)	County/Counties & Places	price reductions (directly enforced)	price reductions (indirectly enforced)	(attempted) expropriations	(attempted) stopping of exports	attacks on property	clashes of rioters and law enforcers	military deployed	fatal injuries/ fatalities	arrests	(attempted) prisoner liberations	reported in Journal issue dated	Notes
4th Oct	Leicestershire; Ashby-de-la-Zouch											11th Oct; p. 3	minor disturbance
4th-9th Oct	Derbyshire/ Leicestershire; in/near Castle Donington			✓	✓	✓	✓			41-43		11th Oct; p. 3	Battle of Donington
7th Oct	Nottinghamshire; Barton			✓								11th Oct; p. 3	-
9th Oct	Wiltshire; Chippenham					✓	✓					18th Oct; p. 3	date estimated
13th Oct	Leicestershire; Leicester			✓	✓		✓					18th Oct; p. 3	-
23rd Oct	North Yorkshire; Scarborough			✓								25th Oct; p. 1	-

Date(s)	County/Counties & Places	price reductions (directly enforced)	price reductions (indirectly enforced)	(attempted) expropriations	(attempted) stopping of exports	attacks on property	clashes of rioters and law enforcers	military deployed	fatal injuries/ fatalities	arrests	(attempted) prisoner liberations	reported in Journal issue dated	Notes
before 18th Oct	Gloucester-shire; Pitchcombe	✓		✓		✓	✓	✓	1	13		25th Oct; p. 3	-
between 13th and 19th Oct	Northampton-shire; Desborough				✓							25th Oct; p. 3	-
N/A	Somerset; near Frome			✓		✓	✓		1			4th Oct; p. 4	'others cannot recover'
N/A	Wiltshire; Bradford-on-Avon			✓								4th Oct; p. 4	-
N/A	Wiltshire; Trowbridge			✓								4th Oct; p. 4	-
N/A	Warwick-shire; N/A				✓		✓	✓	8			18th Oct; p. 1	-
N/A	Warwickshire; near/in Stratford-Upon-Avon	✓										18th Oct; p. 1	-

Bibliography

Newspapers

The Leicester and Nottingham Journal; 4th October 1766; Issue 692.

The ... Journal; 11th October 1766; Issue 693.

The ... Journal; 18th October 1766; Issue 694.

The ... Journal; 25th October 1766; Issue 695.

The ... Journal; 1st November 1766; Issue 696.

Dictionaries

Johnson, Samuel (1768): *A Dictionary of the English Language: In which the Words are deduced from their Originals, Explained in their Different Meanings, Authorized by the Names of the Writers in whose Works they are found*; W.G. Jones; Dublin.

Walker, John (1828): *A Critical Pronouncing Dictionary and Expositor of the English Language*; Collins and Hannay; New York.

Worcester, J.E. (ed./1835): *Johnson's and Walker's English Dictionaries combined – Johnson's English Dictionary, as improved by Todd, and abridged by Chalmers, with Walker's Pronouncing Dictionary combined, to which is added Walker's Key to the Classical Pronunciation of Greek, Latin and Scripture proper Names*; Nathan Hale/Desilver, Thomas, and Company; Boston/Philadelphia.

Edited Sources & Literature

Beckett; John V. (a) (1990): *The Agricultural Revolution*; Basil Blackwell; Oxford.

Beckett; John V. (b) (ed./2006): *A Centenary History of Nottingham*; Phillimore; Chichester.

Brenner, Robert (1976): 'Agrarian Class Struggle and Economic Development in Pre-Industrial Europe'; in: *Past & Present*; Issue 70; pp. 30-75.

Bryson, Emrys (1983): *Portrait of Nottingham*; Robert Hale; London.

Deering, Charles (1970): *The History of Nottingham*; S.R. Publishers; East Ardsley.

Emsley, Clive (2010): *Crime and Society in England 1750-1900*; Longman; Harlow.

Field, Henry (ed./1884): *The Date Book of remarkable and memorable events connected with Nottingham and its Neighbourhood*; Vol. 2: '1750-1884'; Nottingham.

Halhead, Henry (1650): *Inclosure thrown open: or, Depopulation depopulated. Not by spades and mattocks; but, by the word of God, the laws of the land, and solid arguments...*; Ja. Cottrel; London.

Hobsbawm, Eric (a) (1952): 'The Machine Breakers'; in: *Past & Present*; Issue 1; pp. 50-70.

Hobsbawm; Eric (b) (1964): *The Age of Revolution – Europe 1789-1848*; Weidenfeld & Nicholson; London.

Kayne, David (1987): *The Darwen County History Series - A History of Nottinghamshire*; Phillimore; Oxford.

Macdonald, Janet (2006): *Feeding Nelson's Navy – The True Story of Food at Sea in the Georgian Era*; Chatham; London.

Marx, Karl (2005): *Das Kapital – Kritik der politischen Ökonomie*; Vol. 1: ‚Der Produktionsprozess des Kapitals'; Parkland; Köln.

May, Trevor (1997): *An Economic and Social History of Britain 1760-1990*; Longman; Harlow.

Nottingham City Council; *History of the Council House*; http://www.nottinghamcity.gov.uk/article/23273/The-history-of-the-Council-House (retrieved 20th October 2014).

O'Brien, Jo: *Women's Liberation in Labour History – A case study from Nottingham*; Spokesman Pamphlet No. 24; Nottingham.

Orwell, George (2000): *Homage to Catalonia*; Penguin; London.

Pinchbeck, Ivy (1981): *Women Workers and the Industrial Revolution 1750-1850*; Virago; London.

Rich, E.E./Wilson, C.H. (a) (eds./1967): *The Cambridge Economic History of Europe*; Vol. 4: 'The Economy of Expanding Europe in the sixteenth and seventeenth centuries'; Cambridge University Press; Cambridge.

Rudé, George (1959): *The Crowd in the French Revolution*; Oxford University Press; London.

Thompson; E.P. (1991): *The Making of the English Working Class*; Penguin; London.

Wollstonecraft; Mary (2004): *A Vindication of the Rights of Woman*; Penguin; London.

To the Castle!

Nottingham's crowds in the 1831 Reform Riots

Introduction

> *'I'm talking about the most significant programme of empowerment by a British government since the great reforms of the 19th Century. The biggest shake up of our democracy since 1832, when the Great Reform Act redrew the boundaries of British democracy [...].'*[166]

As in this ludicrous speech by the soon-to-be-forgotten Nick Clegg, the so called Great Reform Act was repeatedly referred to and glamourized in the campaigns leading up to the referendum on the Alternative Vote in 2011. The latter will be of little long term consequence, although some had pinned rather astounding hopes[167] on this rather feeble attempt by the Lib Dems and a few others to adjust some aspects of the Westminster playground. Nevertheless some of the rhetoric used in the run-up to the referendum briefly drew public attention onto the 1832 Reform Act.

This provided a welcome backdrop for People's Histreh's project of taking a close look at aspects of the early 1830s Reform Bill Crisis, especially at those events which became known as the Reform Riots.[168]

We did this from a local perspective, examining the riots in Nottingham which followed the rejection of the Reform Bill in the House of Lords in October 1831. It looks into the questions of who the rioting persons were, and what motivated them to engage in their direct action.

The history of Nottingham can be depicted as a long history of social struggles, which were often fuelled by the economic distress of the town's inhabitants (see 1.1.-1.4.).

This interpretation formed the basis of two core theses: stating firstly that, as on numerous other occasions, crowds in the Reform Riots consisted primarily of persons who can be defined as members of the working

166 See BBC News.

167 See Bragg.

168 See Pearce; p. 207: After the riots in Bristol (see 2.5.) this term was coined by Tories.

classes;[169] and secondly, that their actions were motivated by more than just disappointed enthusiasm for the Reform Bill.

The decision to examine said research questions by testing the two core theses was taken at an early stage of the research process. It had been tempting to stick to classic and comfortable patterns of interpretation, and analyse the Reform Bill Crisis as a tame version of the fierce clashes in France between a rising bourgeoisie, aided by a working class 'tail'[170], and an aristocracy clinging on to their privileges. However, this would oversimplify the complex issues and therefore distort any findings. It would require most extensive deliberations to sufficiently analyse how the working, middle and ruling classes constituted and constantly transformed each other in the socioeconomic processes leading up to the Reform Act of 1832. Therefore no attempt was made to engage in such a mammoth project, but the focus was rather placed on a specific group's actions during the Reform Bill Crisis, i.e. those rioters who fought in October 1831 in the town of Nottingham and its neighbourhood.

Accounts of the Reform Bill Crisis are plentiful, especially regarding the proceedings within Westminster. Even though there are also numerous accounts of the riots in Nottingham, the rioters themselves have rarely been described and debated in some detail. A relatively brief article by Thomis, Preston and Wigley aimed to do so, identifying but not rectifying the problem of a distinct:

> '[...] vagueness about the participants in the riots, who have always been "rioters" rather than actual people with a real identity, a crowd of people rather than individuals who make up a crowd.'[171]

In a more recently published article Beckett discussed the rioters' identities more thoroughly, as well as looking into possible motivations for

---

169 The term 'classes' rather than 'class' is used to reflect the divisions among those who were yet to become proletarians. See Hobsbawm (b); p. 120: Class does not define an isolated group of persons, but rather a system of horizontal and vertical relations, expressing differences and similarities but also social functions of exploitation, power and subjection. See Holstun; pp. 96/107: The social relation expressed by the term class is primary one of exploitation taking differing forms in different historical situations. Exploitation and resistance against it can always be seen as forms of class struggle/class war, even if a class consciousness in the sense of a shared consciousness of one's position within the predominant mode of production has not yet developed or has not been adopted. Even though for Holstun class consciousness is the necessary precondition for using the category class, for him it is already a form of class consciousness if someone acts according to her/his position within the mode of production, even though that may not be consciously reflected.

170 Thompson; pp. 216-7.

171 Thomis/Preston/Wigley; p. 82.

their actions. In doing so, he went beyond the usual patterns of stereotyping the rioters for example as 'hooligans' intent on 'plunder'. However, Beckett barely discussed clues towards the rioters' identities other than those that can be found in prosecution records, thereby for example failing to acknowledge the role of women in the riots. Furthermore, he largely accepted the depiction of events presented during the trials, thus for instance adopting the prosecution's focus on identifying ringleaders. Regarding the rioters' motives, Beckett did not really discuss the possibility that the rioters' actions may have been motivated by more than just the immediate issue of the rejected Reform Bill, i.e. anything other than a desire to 'chase anti-reformers' and Tories.[172] Therefore Beckett is unable to provide possible explanations for a number of events during the Reform Riots.

Despite the legitimate critique of Thomis, Preston and Wigley, the terms 'rioters' and 'crowds' are also used extensively in this book. However, the following deliberations go further than most other accounts of the Reform Riots by looking not only at the crowds as bodies of people, but also by looking into the crowds, and taking a few glimpses at some of the individuals within them. Furthermore a historical framework is provided by contextualising the political and socioeconomic circumstances of rioters' actions. Due to the absence of any sources outlining the rioters' motives from their own points of view, this debate has to be based on circumstantial evidence only and deduced indirectly, for example from an extensive examination of the rioters' targets.

In order to do so, a number of sources have been used. To start with, there were various general works on the history of Nottingham, none of which would be complete without at least mentioning the Reform Riots and the destruction of Nottingham Castle. Noteworthy examples for such works include Field's *Date Book...*, Bryson's *Portrait of Nottingham* or an article by Gray in the *Transactions of the Thoroton Society....* Classic descriptions of the town such as in Defoe's *A Tour Through the Whole Island...* or Deering's *The History of Nottingham*, both written in the seventeenth century, proved to be entertaining and useful. Thomis' *Politics and Society in Nottingham 1785-1835* was indispensable, although also often infuriating. Specific information on and interpretations of the Reform Bill Crisis were found in works of Pearce, Dinwiddy and Wright, but it would be an outrage not to mention Thompson's epic *The Making of the English Working Class*. Hernon, Thomis, Preston and Wigley provided some information of the Reform Riots in Nottingham and other parts of Britain. Edited sources and summaries in Wylly or Fellows and Freeman provided detailed accounts of the events in Nottingham and reflected the military's

---

[172] Beckett; p. 122.

perception of the rioters and their actions. Brilliant fun and an invaluable source for the Nottingham riots and their aftermath are Hicklin's hilarious *History of Nottingham Castle...*, written only five years after the events, and the carefully edited *...Diaries of the Fourth Duke of Newcastle-Under-Lyne...* the latter providing crucial evidence for all aspects discussed in this text. The main body of information about the Reform Riots in Nottingham, their aftermath and the rioting persons was excerpted from various local newspapers. Further evidence could be found in other primary sources, notably the *...Calendar of the Prisoners...*, an extensive list of those who were to be put on trial before the Special Assize in 1832, and the various statements, for example by Magistrates and the town clerk, recorded in *A report of the evidence given before the commissioners....*

To shed some light into the research questions by testing the two core theses required not only a description and debate of the riots themselves, but also extensive deliberations of their historical context. Therefore the first chapter sketches the riotous reputation of Nottingham's inhabitants, who were used to engage in direct action (1.1.). The following subchapters outline the town's and its industries' development in the late eighteenth and early nineteenth centuries (1.2/1.3.) and living and working conditions of the people of Nottingham (1.4.). Various aspects of the long and complex struggles aiming at parliamentary reform up to the rejection of the second Reform Bill in the House of Lords are depicted in 1.5. The Reform Riots are examined in the second chapter, with an extensive, chronological description of events in the town of Nottingham and its neighbourhood (2.1.-2.4.) as well as a brief summary of events in other parts of Britain (2.5.). Subchapter 3.1. focuses on the prosecution of the rioters and 3.2. on criticisms of the conduct of the town's officials during the riots. At the end of the third chapter events leading up to the 1832 Reform Act and its consequences are briefly outlined (3.3.). Chapter four centres on the rioters themselves, initially by trying to identify patterns in the descriptions of rioting crowds, referring to concepts of crowd psychology drawn up at the end of the nineteenth century (4.1.). In 4.2. the available evidence is analysed as to whether it provides information about the individuals engaged in the direct action. After debating who the rioters might have been, their possible motives are discussed by critically examining the available empirical evidence as well as interpretations of historians and the rioters' contemporaries. Finally, the conclusions are followed by a number of appendices, for example presenting the excerpted empirical data in various tables, and providing maps, images and quotations from primary sources.

1. The Setting

1.1. The reputation of Nottingham's crowds

> *'Through most of the eighteenth and nineteenth centuries, the characteristic sounds in Nottingham were the noise of jeering crowds, the whine of musket balls and the smashing of glass.'* [173]

Nottingham has been described as a 'Banner town, always at or near the front of Reform Movements'.[174]

Its inhabitants had a distinct reputation for being a 'combustible and dangerous mob', living up to a long tradition of political and religious dissent, 'accustomed to taking the law into their own hands when the occasion demanded it'.[175] Defying patriarchal standards, women actively participated in, and often led, protests and riots.[176]

The few constables were unable to effectively suppress the town's inhabitants, even less so whenever the locals were reinforced by people from the county, for instance during fairs and markets. If crowds resorted to various forms of direct action, usually whenever living conditions became unbearable, riotous events often ended with 'the sabre-swishing military' dispersing crowds, repeatedly resulting 'in a few corpses being added to the rubble'.[177]

Even though the overwhelming majority of the people of Nottingham were not eligible to vote, many took an active part in parliamentary politics

---

173 Bryson; p. 127.

174 Wyncoll; p. 19. See Bryson; p. 90: Notably in Nottingham's turbulent history is the emergence of Luddism which eventually tied up more troops in the Midlands than Wellington took with him to fight the Peninsular War.

175 Thomis (a); pp. 1-2/7: Nottingham's inhabitants have been described as people who often 'thought for themselves and formed their opinions without regard to title or wealth.'

176 See idem (b); pp. 22-3: Better known examples for women's engagement in protests and riots occurred in 1812 when on various riotous occasions people took on the role of 'Lady Ludd'. See O'Brien; pp. 4/8-10: If women's political activities are mentioned at all, the majority of historical accounts only refer to women's involvement in food riots. Ignoring e.g. the activities of women trade unionists is a strategy to reaffirm patriarchal notions as it seems more 'acceptable for women to act over food prices because this accords with the idea that they are, and always have been, domestic centred.' See also *Damn your charity...*; chapter 5.

177 Bryson; p. 129; Thomis (a); p. 7. See Beckett (b); pp. 291-2: Nottingham became 'the first sizeable English town to be awarded its own barracks for the permanent quartering of troops.'

by engaging in election campaigns.[178] In early nineteenth century Nottingham, the militaristic language still used in modern parliamentary politics had a very real meaning as election campaigns were often fought in the very sense of the word. Pitched 'battles between hired armies [...] were part and parcel of the Nottingham election scene.'[179]

In a nutshell, economical despair, politics and religion fuelled social tensions in Nottingham and riots occurred regularly, averaging one a year at the turn of the century.[180]

However, by the end of the 1820s the town had lost much of its tumultuous reputation, with inhabitants even keeping 'orderliness' during the harsh winter of 1829-30. By 1830 Nottingham was even referred to as a peaceful town, a description that was not going to be used after October 1831, when the 'spirit' of Nottingham and Derby was often referred to with anxiety.[181]

1.2. The 'Garden Town' 'sinks into slime'

In the mid eighteenth century, Nottingham was described as a 'one of the most pleasant and beautiful towns in England',[182] when:

---

178 Bryson; p. 127; Thomis (a); p. 143: The electorate consisted of the town's burgesses, i.e. eligible males, for instance 40s freeholders, those who had been made honorary burgesses, or people who completed an apprenticeship. The latter criterion made it possible for a relatively large number of framework knitters to vote, making the Nottingham electorate a mixture of male property owners as well as male members of the working classes. The size of the electorate before 1832 is hard to estimate. According to the rather vague figures suggested by Thomis it was slightly less than ten per cent of the total population, a comparatively high proportion of inhabitants. See Nottingham Corporation; p. 9: for detailed descriptions how a male person could get the status of a 'free-man'. See Beckett (a); p. 115: '[Nottingham] was governed by a dissenting, whig corporation [...] since the 1790s.' See idem (b); pp. 193-4: 'Whig hold on power remained unbroken' until 1835.

179 Bryson; pp. 129-30. See Beckett (b); pp. 289-90 for a description of an election riot in 1790.

180 Field; p. 225: During a military ceremony in 1799, an army chaplain referred to the remark of a fellow 'gentleman' who had stated that 'he had lived seventeen years in the town of Nottingham, and during that period there had been seventeen riots'. See also Appendix XIV.

181 Thomis/Preston/Wigley; p. 88/95. See *Journal*; 15th October 1831; 15th October 1831: This was one of the *Journal's* major concerns after the Reform Riots: 'we [fear] for the credit of our town'.

182 Defoe; p. 451. See ibid; pp. 451-6: Defoe's description of the town is quite charming. It does not only allow a glimpse at mid-seventeenth century Nottingham but also its visitor. Defoe wrote primarily about the castle and the beer, leaving the reader speculating whether his stay entailed nothing but arrival and getting drunk at 'Ye Olde Trip To Jerusalem'.

> '[...] the back-to-back slums had not even begun to appear; when the Meadows each spring were a carpet of crocus, and the population was not too large [...]; and when the stocking industry was scarcely in its infancy'.[183]

However, the question whether mid seventeenth century Nottingham really was such an idyllic, beautiful 'garden town' is here less relevant than the process by which Nottingham 'began to sink rapidly into slime' within a few decades.[184]

Whilst most of the towns which became industrial centres grew not only in population, but also in area,[185] Nottingham did not. Indeed, the population had outgrown the unchanged medieval town boundaries well before the 1830s. At the beginning of the nineteenth century 8,000 houses were crammed in 132 streets, off which ran 308 courts and alleyways, housing in 1801 28,801 inhabitants on the same perimeter (of one and 3/4 miles)[186] where in 1739 only 9,890 people had lived.[187] By 1831 the population was to further increase to 50,000.[188] With a statistical average of just over ten square yards for each person, the centre of Nottingham had a higher population density than London or indeed any other place in the British Isles.[189]

Nottingham was surrounded by areas to which various protagonists claimed 'inviolable' property rights. On the west the expansion of the town was blocked by the Duke of Newcastle's Nottingham Park and Lord Middleton's Wollaton Park. On the east there was Colwick parish, owned by the Musters family. To the North and the South were the common fields

---

183 Gray; p. 30.

184 Bryson; p. 75/83: 'From a garden city [Nottingham] turned into a slum second only to Bombay throughout the whole Empire.'

185 Gray; p. 30.

186 Kayne; pp. 93/98: These figures refer to census data, collected by town officials noting names, gender, age, occupation, etc. of persons present in a specific house at the time of their visit. That this imprecise method was far more reliable than previous ones demonstrates that, whilst all empirical data has be treated with caution, especially figures deriving from historical demography can only be taken as indicators illustrating trends.

187 Deering; pp. 12-3. See Bryson; pp. 74/83: By 1750 the population had only increased to 11,000. See Thomis (a); p. 2: He estimates the number of inhabitants to have been 17,000 in 1779.

188 Bryson; p. 99; Thomis (a); p. 2. See Beckett (b); pp. 191-3; Lowe/Richards; p. 25: The bulk of the population increase occurred in the 1820s.

189 Thomis (a); p. 24: There was some migration of 'better-off' workers to suburbs like New Radford or Hyson Green, but that was little relief. See Beckett (b); pp. 204-6: The transformation of Nottingham's town centre into 'an industrial slum' resulted in the middle classes resorting to 'an orderly retreat into suburban enclaves designed for their own benefit.'

and meadows, which have been described as 'the biggest stumbling block of all'.[190]

The common lands were not quite as common as the name suggests. Instead, they were mostly controlled by burgesses and freeholders, who vigorously defended their users' rights. A frequent though paradoxical argument by the opponents of enclosure were health reasons, as they claimed that public interest demanded the preservation of Nottingham's open spaces. But it can be assumed that opposition to enclosure was primarily upheld for economic reasons. Some of those who held users' rights on the commons were renting them out as grazing spaces and others were landlords who wanted to keep their overcrowded town properties occupied.[191]

As the population rapidly expanded, Market Square became a 'muddy slough' and its side streets 'filled with back-to-back houses springing up like clusters of dirty mushrooms'. By the 1830s and 1840s the whole town had become 'one mighty prison of bricks and mortar'. The streets were narrow, dangerous and mostly unpaved, filled with 'pools of filthy water or most extended dung heaps'.[192]

> 'Hardly a day passed [...] without some unfortunate being crushed in Sheep Lane (Market Street now), either trapped between wall and wagon wheels or pounded to death as some terrified bullock from the cattle sales in the square stampeded through the chaos.'[193]

The Nottingham Corporation took no responsibility for social or infrastructural matters other than 'providing law and order', and leaving the 'dirt to accumulate.' Attempts at improvements were scrapped due to costs. Where infrastructural programmes were finally realised, they were private schemes, in which the corporation was – if at all – only one

---

190 Welch (a); p. 8: 'Nottingham was prevented from expanding partly by big landowners and partly by freemen clinging to their privileges over the commonlands [...].' See Bryson; pp. 83-4: Unlike Welch, Bryson only refers to the common lands when he describes how expansion could have 'saved' Nottingham from 'throttling itself'. He is not the only one who does not discuss the areas blocked by Newcastle's, Middleton's or the Musters' property claims (e.g. Gray and Thomis fail to do so as well). Bryson does state that the poorest inhabitants were also opponents of enclosures as they 'queued up in the hope of winning one of the 250 "burgess parts" of arable land' which became available on a sort of lottery basis. See Thomis (a); pp. 28/122-3/125-6: The issue of enclosure was 'the most consistently recurring theme of all Nottingham elections, local and parliamentary'.

191 Ibid; pp. 4/24/124-6. See Bryson; p. 99: He estimates slum landlords' rents totalled £40,000 a year.

192 Ibid; pp. 84/98.

193 Ibid; p. 85.

subscriber.[194] The attitude of the Corporation as to what constituted their public duties can be exemplified by a statement by the town clerk, a Mr Enfield who, asked in 1833 whether there had been 'any very great public improvements', replied that the 'House of Correction has been improved [and] enlarged.'[195]

Slum property owners were erecting the maximum number of houses on a minimum of space, many built back to back:[196]

> 'In Nottingham there are in all 11,000 houses, of which between 7,000 and 8,000 are built back to back with a rear party wall so that no through ventilation is possible.'[197]

Such dwellings were a common sight in most industrial towns of the time, arranged in narrow courts closed at both ends, which were entered by yard-wide tunnels eight feet high and twenty to thirty feet long. Construction was bad and sanitation crude, with a characteristic open sewer running down the centre of a court. In 1812 300 of these enclosed courts with open sewers existed in Nottingham.[198] Typical houses consisted of two or sometimes three rooms on successive storeys, each eleven feet square, with a tiny space for food and coal under the stairs. Some had cellar dwellings in the sandstone beneath. None of the houses had a damp course. At one end of the courts was a group of privies – one for the use of up to thirty people, often situated underneath bedrooms. Many of these houses were also workshops, 'thumping with the noise of frameworking or lace dressing'. Certain stages in the lace production required high temperatures and a humid atmosphere, resulting in houses being heated by stoves, hot water and steam, which 'made the thin porous walls alive with vermin'.[199]

---

194 Thomis (a); pp. 4/24. See Beckett (b); p. 194: '[The] corporation was most likely to spend money on improvements beneficial to itself, such as the £14,000 it laid out in 1814-15 reconstructing the Exchange. See ibid; pp. 193-4; Nottingham Corporation; pp. 4-18; Thomis (a); pp. 114-42 for the structure and history of the Nottingham Corporation in the late eighteenth and early nineteenth centuries.

195 Nottingham Corporation; pp. 37/43: Pressed on the matter he also named the New Exchange building. After being told that it was 'a private building for the use of the Corporation', he explained that it was of public benefit as it was 'ornamental and beautiful.'

196 See Beckett (b); pp. 200-4 on housing development in the town's centre.

197 Engels (b); p. 78. See ibid; p. 94.

198 Thomis (a); p. 24. Beckett (b) suggests that it were not so much the buildings which were 'inadequate', but that the 'poor quality of the environment' was due to the absence of necessary facilities.

199 Bryson; p. 98; Thomis (a); pp. 3/24. See Nottingham Corporation; p. 163: 4,283 persons shared 'fifty-two sets of privies thirty-six of them having habitations over them, and the number of seats in the privies, one hundred and fifty, or one to every twenty-eight persons.'

Living in such conditions, 'survival had replaced comfort as the aim of working people.'[200]

1.3. Industries in Nottingham

In the 1830s Nottingham was already a rapidly industrialising town with a favourable infrastructure. However, many of the images conjured up by the term Industrial Revolution, such as huge factories with large chimneys, or steaming locomotives, were not yet part of the picture.[201]

The town's primary industrial output consisted of various textile commodities. By 1812 an estimated half of the adult population was operating lace machines or stocking frames; many others worked in allied occupations. In the 1830s the hosiery industry was still dominant, but the town had already become a centre for lace production.[202] Part of the latter industries' expansion was due to various technological advances, especially the bobbin-net machine invented by Heathcoat, which meant that from 1809 'the production of lace was greatly simplified, and the demand increased proportionately in consequence of the diminished cost'.[203] The new industry was an 'offshoot of the hosiery trade – hence its establishment in the old frame-work knitting centres.' It created 'an entirely new field of employment for an enormous number of women and children',[204] drawing in many women workers from the surrounding areas.[205]

In 1823 the expiration of the patent on Heathcoat's machine led to a spectacular boom in the lace industry as many seized the opportunity and 'entered the lace business as master lacemakers (or twist net makers).' A very brief period of 'amazing prosperity' began which 'became known as that of the twist net fever'.[206] Profits and incomes soared to unprecedented

---

200 Thomis (a); p. 25.

201 Beckett (b); pp. 195-200; Bryson; p. 84; Gray; p. 31. See Kayne; pp. 88-9: A railway link was not opened until 1839. However, Nottingham already had an effective infrastructure for the transportation of large quantities of commodities as in 1796 the Nottingham Canal linked the Cromford Canal with the Trent, 'turning the borough into in inland port'.

202 Thomis (a); pp. 13-4: Woollen and silk commodities were also produced in Nottingham even though those trades were mainly associated with Derby and Leicester.

203 Engels (b); pp. 55-6.

204 Pinchbeck; p. 209.

205 O'Brien; p. 5.

206 Gray; p. 34. See Gaunt (a); p. 172: Newcastle noted in 1824 that 'The Town & trade has never been in a more thriving condition' and that there are 'Many foreigners in the Town buying lace'. See Lowe/Richards; p. 25: Here the 'fever' is described as 'lace mania.' In the 1820s the number of bobbin-net machines increased five-fold to 5,000. The boom resulted in a dramatic population increase in Nottingham and the surrounding parishes Sneinton, Lenton, Basford and Bulwell.

levels whilst unemployment was low, even though the population increased dramatically. The boom was followed by the bust of 1825,[207] causing the workers' plight to return, 'grimmer than in 1812."[208] From the late 1820s until the eve of the Reform Riots the cycle of boom and bust in the lace industry was to be repeated several times.[209]

Whilst the lace trade was constantly undergoing violent fluctuations, by 1809 the hosiery industry had entered a forty-year period of almost permanent depression. The industry had a long history in Nottingham with the town having been its centre since the eighteenth century. The long lasting depression had a complex set of reasons, of which Thomis gives a detailed account. Contributing factors were the long lasting wars with Revolutionary and subsequently Napoleonic France, as trading with overseas markets declined and at times collapsed. Furthermore, the stocking trade suffered by a change in fashion as trousers became more popular. However, according to Thomis these circumstances only 'brought to a head evils from which the trade had long been suffering'. For him overproduction lay at the heart of the on-going depression. With the growing population of the town, the production of stockings had increased steadily. Also, new designs of stocking frames resulted in the market being flooded with the so called cut-up stockings, worse in quality but much cheaper as they required less labour. With ever more people trying to earn a living in the trade, hence producing ever more and cheaper stockings, prices fell dramatically, making it necessary to produce even more to compensate for the decreasing income. Between 1812 and 1844 – years of static export trade and only modestly increased home demand – the number of stocking frames rose from 30,000 to 50,000.[210]

Despite various innovations in the design of the industry's principal machine, the stocking-frame, one remarkable aspect of the hosiery industry was its basically static nature. The frame's basic design had been unchanged since Tudor times, with its motive power supplied by its operator.[211] The production and distribution relations not only within the hosiery but also the majority of the lace industry were also essentially unchanged since sixteenth and seventeenth centuries, the early days of the spread of the capitalist mode of production.[212]

The bulk of the industrial output of the town was still produced by the so-called domestic or putting-out system. The majority of textile workers

[207] Beckett (b); pp. 206-8; Bryson; pp. 93-4; Gray; p. 34; Thomis (a); pp. 2-3.
[208] Bryson; p. 94: Poverty and starvation took up their double handed grip again.
[209] Ibid; p. 94; Gray; p. 34.
[210] Thomis (a); pp. 6/29-33.
[211] Ibid; pp. 32-3.
[212] Braudel; p. 620; Holderness; pp. 106-7.

produced in their own homes, mostly with rented tools, receiving raw materials from and delivering the results of their work to 'merchants who were in the process of becoming employers.'[213]

It would be imprecise to label these merchants capitalists, whilst the workers were not yet proletarians. Although the majority of the latter did not own any means of production, they did not sell their labour on the market, but sold commodities produced by their own labour on rented frames, often to the very person owning the frames. In this domestic system, workers were even more vulnerable than factory workers. It was much harder to organise[214] in a system where workers were scattered in small production units competing with each other, rather than being concentrated in large workshops or factories. Furthermore, any slump in demand hit the artisans first and hardest. Whilst they had to rent frames and finance the other raw materials necessary for the production process, usually by piling up debts, they were unable to sell or forced to sell the finished textiles at much lower rates whenever demand dropped. Domestic workers' debts could therefore easily spiral out of control. To make matters worse, these production relations made it even easier for hosiers not to pay framework knitters the full rates due, for instance because of allegedly bad quality of the finished commodities.[215]

That such a system, defying common clichés about the industrial revolution, was anything but atypical lead Thompson to conclude that the 'factory hands, [...] far from being the "eldest children of the industrial revolution", were late arrivals.'[216]

In short, at the time of the Reform Riots, Nottingham's industrial output did not yet come out of factories but rather out of working people's homes. Their occupants lived 'a life of grinding, stupefying toil' and their misery ran 'like a dirty thread through Nottingham's industrial life.'[217]

1.4. Living and working conditions

In January 1831, nine months before the Reform Riots, the Duke of Newcastle depicted the economic situation of the town very optimistically,

---

213 Hobsbawm (a); pp. 36-7. See Beckett (b); p. 318: for a description of the organisation of the hosiery trade.

214 Bryson; p. 87; Thomis (a); pp. 28/32-3/50-76.

215 Clay; p. 9; Thirsk; pp. 170-1; Thomis (a); p. 29.

216 Thompson; p. 211. See Thomis (a); pp. 35-6/47-8: Factory production and the large scale application of steam power in Nottingham's hosiery industry did not start until the 1850s, and it came along with a diversification of Nottingham's trades. 'In any debate on the merits and demerits of the "factory-system" it must be conceded that it was the only possible salvation left to hosiery and that its belated arrival was a tragedy to a whole generation of framework knitters.' The lace industry had been moving towards factory production faster than hosiery.

217 Bryson; p. 87/128.

writing that 'the people in this county generally are in full work & at good wages (2s a day) at Nottingham the trade has never been better'.[218]

His claim was one of total ignorance of working peoples' plight, as in 1830 an estimated half of the town's inhabitants were in receipt of poor relief. Even though economic despair, especially of the hosiery workers, was by no means a new phenomenon and the phrase 'as poor as a stockinger' had allegedly been used since the 1740s,[219] Thomis claims that hosiery workers suffered a deterioration of living standards in the period 1785-1835.[220]

One indicator which helps to piece together a picture of the living conditions of working people in Nottingham is their average life expectancy. For the whole town it has been stated as being just over twenty-two, seven years lower than the national average. In some areas it was fourteen or fifteen, in parts of St Anns 'it touched eleven', the lowest rate recorded in the British Empire.[221]

Another indicator is the level of incomes. Describing and analysing the development of workers' incomes, especially for those toiling in the domestic industries, is complicated by various methodological problems,[222] not least as gender bias usually distorts the picture. The income generated by all family members' economic activities is usually only accredited to the labour of the patriarch, ignoring that in working persons' households everyone worked, regardless of gender or age, with women not only being engaged in producing commodities but also in unpaid reproductive work.[223]

---

218 Gaunt (a); p. 74.

219 Bryson; pp. 87/94; Gray; p. 34; Thomis (a); p. 14. See Beckett (b); pp. 208-11 for a brief description of charitable institutions, workhouses, etc.

220 Thomis (a); pp. 14/18: Thomis choice of the year 1835 is an entirely arbitrary date, for there was to be 'no improvement for a further twenty years.'

221 Bryson; p. 99; Kayne; p. 93; Thomis (a); p. 24; Welch (a); p. 14.

222 Thomis (a); pp. 14-5: Not only have seasonal fluctuations to be taken into consideration, but also other factors like the hosier's practice of assigning the available work to the highest possible number of workers to maximise income generated by frame rents. Employers also retained a discretionary power to vary payment according to their perception of the quality of the work and make deductions for wastage and error. Furthermore the figures available must be treated with care as employers tended to cite the most favourable and trade union committees the worst figures available. 'The manufacturer believed the stockinger to be a liar; the stockinger believed the manufacturer to be a cheat.'

223 Shepard; pp. 83-4; Thirsk; pp. 173-4: Thirsk's and Shepard's critique, although made in respect to the historians of a different period are equally valid for many accounts of nineteenth century socioeconomic history. See also O'Brien; p. 4: 'The man was not the family breadwinner. Each member would contribute financially, and each contribution was essential to keep the family from starvation.'

Although he provides a large body of empirical evidence regarding income rates and their long term development, Thomis is an example of the historians who fail to acknowledge that their data is gender biased, at least by admitting that it does not reflect the situation of all workers, but rather that of adult male workers. Thomis claims that hosiery workers' living conditions were not yet desperate in the late eighteenth century, when incomes were said to have been 10s to 12s a week, and in the skilled segments of production as high as 30s. In the 1790s the wars against revolutionary France initially had no negative effect as the military bought huge quantities of commodities. By 1809 this had changed, with enormous consequences for the workers. At the beginning of the period of Luddite unrest even the highest paid labourers, for instance the silk workers, were earning no more than 12s a week, whilst 7s 3d were seen as relatively high incomes compared to other textile workers. In 1826 takings of highly paid workers had further dropped to 9s or 10s a week, in 1827 it was reported that on average eighty hours of work generated as little as 6s to 7s a week for most workers. In the 1830s, hosiery workers' estimated incomes had fallen by 30-50 per cent since the beginning of the century.[224] O'Brien refers to female framework knitters earning 2s 6d in the same period, exemplifying the massive gender gap in workers' incomes.[225]

The incomes of lace workers were considerably better. They had briefly risen to astronomical heights in the short-lived boom of 1824-5, when some workers allegedly took home as much as £5 a week. In the following years incomes fell to 24s in 1829, 18s in 1833 and 12s in 1838.[226] Again Thomis fails to mention that for the majority of the, predominantly female,[227] workforce in the lace industry, incomes will have been considerably lower. Pinchbeck refers to reports of women embroidering silk bobbin net shawls, working fourteen hours whilst earning only 1s a day.[228]

Price developments also back up Thomis' claim of deteriorating living standards, as prices soared whilst incomes shrank. It has been suggested that in the years 1792-1832 prices for food and other necessities of life rose by up to 150 per cent. Thomis' rather cautious estimate – which would nevertheless have been disastrous – is of prices rising by about a quarter compared with levels in 1785, whilst incomes fell by about a third.[229]

---

224 Thomis (a); pp. 15-19.

225 O'Brien; pp. 6-7.

226 Bryson; p. 87; Thomis (a); pp. 15-19: 'As with the hosiery workers, wages were falling, and [...] pressures of longer hours and harder work were [increasing].'

227 O'Brien; p. 6: '[...] the census of 1844 revealed that in all the branches of the lace industry in Great Britain there were 15,876 women over twenty, 6,040 girls under twenty, to compare with only 5,373 men and 1,082 boys.'

228 Pinchbeck; p. 211.

229 Thomis (a); pp. 19-20. See ibid; pp. 20-1 for descriptions of various food and coal riots.

In addition to the expenses for food etc., the overwhelming majority of Nottingham's textile workers had to pay frame rents to the hosiers, which amounted to about one sixth of weekly incomes.[230] In times of unemployment the frame was lost, or those renting it were further spiralling into debt.[231]

Taking the figures for incomes and expenses, Thomis' claim of declining living standards can be exemplified in the increasing length of a working day. The number of working hours necessary to afford clothes, housing and food, not mentioning the additional hours of necessary reproductive work, have been estimated at ten hours in 1760, fourteen in 1821 and sixteen in 1835.[232]

A typical workers' diet contained nothing but 'old milk, barley-bread and potatoes. At times, workers could not afford bread or potatoes'. In 1845 the diet of workers in Nottingham was described as 'low and precarious', consisting of bread, potatoes and herrings, all 'other or better articles [being] strangers to the tables of the poor'.[233]

Thomis concludes that between the 1780s and the 1830s there:

> '[...] was not a uniform decline, either in its impact or its timing, [however] it is clear that during the final decade of the period Nottingham was in almost perpetual depression, alleviated by only very transitionary periods of buoyancy, and that distress was extremely severe and very widespread.'[234]

One group of workers who had to suffer exceptionally were children, especially those toiling in cottages and small workshops. Sixteen hours a day were a normal workload, with child workers being:

> '[...] kept up until 11 pm or midnight, boys of five winding yarn, little girls standing on stools [...] as they stitched away at seams. Mothers would pin them on their knees, giving them a slap on the head if they fell asleep before their stint was finished.'[235]

---

230 Ibid; p. 28.
231 Bryson; p. 78.
232 Thomis (a); pp. 17-8.
233 Ibid; p. 21.
234 Ibid; p. 26.
235 Bryson; pp. 85-6: Child labour was common in many industries. Children aged four or even younger were working alongside their families in the textile industry, others toiled in coal pits from the age of six, or worked at brickyards in Mapperley or as sweeping chimneys 'hardening their flesh with vinegar and being encouraged to hurry by their masters lighting a fire in the hearth'.

There has been an intense debate about whether the spread of factory production resulted in an improvement of working conditions, even though it did not lead to a reduction of working hours.[236] That claims of improvements can still be supported by various pieces of evidence, must not be understood as a defence of the horrors of Victorian factory work[237] but rather as a necessary challenge of the romanticised myths[238] of domestic workers' living and working conditions.

In any case, working in the textile industries had drastic consequences. Workers operating stocking frames were said to be identifiable by their physical appearance. They were undergoing rapid physical deterioration from an early age and often had respiratory and digestive organ diseases 'from [their] early association with the cramping frame.'[239]

Under these circumstances it seems highly surprising that in 1834 eighty-four per cent of children were connected – at least officially – to an educational establishment of some sort, mostly Sunday Schools:

> 'Sunday schools were advocated as a factor in promoting social cohesion and as part of the answer to crime, [but] a person, taught to read the Bible might also lay hands upon the Age of Reason or the Rights of Man. If Sunday Schools were intended to keep people in their places, they also gave to some the means of changing places.'[240]

---

[236] Ibid; pp. 98-9; Pinchbeck; p. 307. See ibid; p. 188: In 1833 it was found that 'although the day's work was considered to be twelve hours, the actual practice was to extend that period to sixteen and sometimes eighteen hours [...].'

[237] Engels (b); pp. 203-6; Bryson; pp. 98-9: Also in Nottingham's factories children suffered most, referring to an infamous report a youth in a cotton mill near Lowdham: 'Sick and fainting, supervised by an overseer with a horsewhip, they eked out their miserable existence [...]. [The] children frequently collapsed with fatigue into the machines. Robert Blincoe [...] described seeing a girl of eight whose dress caught in a shaft. She was dragged into the machinery and spun round like a rag doll, her bones cracking and her blood spraying as if from a wrung-out mop.' Thomis (a); pp. 21-3: Even though workers in a factory setting might have been relatively better paid and therefore better fed, Thomis states that they would have been even more prone to respiratory diseases.

[238] See Engels (b); pp. 50-2: This is an example of such an idealised depiction.

[239] Thomis (a); pp. 2-3/22-3.

[240] Ibid. See Le Bon; pp. 85/88/98: He feared the 'acquisition of knowledge [...] a sure method of driving a man to revolt' and wrote that 'the worst enemies of society, the anarchists, are recruited among the prize-winners of schools'. See Thomis (a); p. 9: Sunday Schools also provided minimal education to adults and Nottingham has been suggested as the birthplace of the Adult School movement. Hoare; pp. 284-8: Although Nottingham's working class Operatives' Libraries were not founded before the latter half of the 1830s, there were limited possibilities for working class people to get their hands on books on the eve of the Reform Riots, e.g. in libraries set up by well-meaning middle class people.

1.5. The struggle for parliamentary reform

In its immediate aftermath, the 'French revolution consolidated old corruption by uniting landowners and manufacturers in a common panic'.[241] But although the downfall of the French Ancien Régime at first revived its British counterpart,[242] the post 1688 class compromise[243] was no longer able to incorporate the drastic socioeconomic transformations without any adjustment. Fast-growing towns like Manchester, Birmingham, Bradford and Leeds had no parliamentary representation, whilst hamlets could send one or even two MPs, often controlled by landed magnates, to Westminster.[244]

By the 1830s the issue of parliamentary reform had for decades been on the agenda of reformists and radicals alike. Many gatherings had taken place and numerous lives been lost, for instance in the Peterloo Massacre on the 16th August 1819, when approximately fifteen died and hundreds were injured as people were slashed and trampled by charging cavalry troopers.[245]

In the prelude to the Reform Bill Crisis 1830-2, parliamentary reform had been an umbrella term for numerous groups and individuals campaigning by various means for very diverse aims and agendas, although male campaigners were virtually unanimous in their determination to withhold the suffrage from women.[246]

The complex debates and internal fault lines within the factions of reformers and radicals were interwoven with the socioeconomic upheaval in Britain, changing power and production relations, as well as shifting the framework of the parliamentary regime.

> 'New interests were clearly not adequately represented in Parliament. The conflict of "court versus country" was to be replaced by conflicts between industry and agriculture, between town and countryside [...], between labour and

241 Thompson; p. 195; Wright; pp. 20-3.

242 Thompson; pp. 216-7.

243 Engels (a); p. 8939 (see MEW volume 22; pp. 301-2): Engels described the outcome of the so called Glorious Revolution as a class compromise between aristocracy, gentry and bourgeoisie. The monarchy continued to exist but parliamentary sovereignty was guaranteed and Parliament was given powers to keep the monarchy in check.

244 Hernon; p. 58. See Thomis (a); pp. 143-68 for details on the parliamentary borough of Nottingham before 1832.

245 Hernon; pp. 28-46; Rudé; pp. 94-5; Thompson; p. 899.

246 See Dinwiddy; p. 15: Apparently James Mill did believe that women should be entitled to the vote, but 'he considered that to put forward such a proposal [...] would retard the cause of political reform by exposing it to ridicule.'

capital. The England of Burke was to become the England of Marx.'[247]

It has been much debated why persons and groups, identified with or identifying themselves as part of the working classes,[248] did pursue parliamentary reform.[249] Dinwiddy argues that this can be partly explained by the ineffectiveness of other strategies as on many occasions direct action had been tried with 'very little positive result'. The issue was intensively and diversely debated, and working class support for parliamentary reform varied hugely in different parts of the country, not least as most proposals offered at best indirect improvements to the lives of the working classes.[250] However, claims of a 'swelling surge towards political change', here to be understood as changes within the framework of parliamentary politics, were not unfounded.[251] It can be assumed that also among working class people in Nottingham quite a few indulged hopes that even moderate parliamentary reform might result in 'an alleviation of suffering', a 'change of fortune' after the slumps that followed the short boom of the 1820s.[252]

Although far from having a coherent agenda, the majority of the local middle classes[253] were supporting moderate parliamentary reform. The Whig dominated Nottingham Corporation attempted 'to lead and give expression' to reformist and radical movements whilst resisting 'any

---

247 Wright; pp. 1-10.

248 Ibid; p. 12: Socioeconomic change always shapes and is in turn shaped by the transformation of class structures. Class in industrialising Britain was, as always, a complex category which has to be differentiated carefully, as Wright illustrates for the working classes where divisions 'ran deep, [for instance] between the domestic and factory workers'. Wright argues that despite the complexity of the category, it was very relevant as 'the simple class model was held by many contemporaries and was a potent catalyst of political change.'

249 See Dinwiddy; pp. 19-30. See Thompson; pp. 909-10: '[...] for the workers of this and the next decade, [the vote] was a symbol whose importance it is difficult for us to appreciate, our eyes dimmed by more than a century of the smog of "two-party parliamentary politics".' According to Thompson the vote had symbolic value and was 'a yet unknown tool' to exercise social control over 'conditions of life and labour.'

250 Dinwiddy; pp. 25/62-7 See Thomis (a); pp. 217-25 for details on local reformers' activities.

251 Bryson; p. 94. See Pearce; p. 151/165-6: There were e.g. mass meetings and marches in support of reform in April and May 1831.

252 Bryson; p. 94; Gray; pp. 31/34.

253 Wright; pp. 12/33-6: Who constituted the middle classes is intensively debated. In the discourse of the time the category was often used synonymously with the equally vague one of 'respectable' people. See Dinwiddy; pp. 55-60 for details on the middle classes and their attitudes towards the bill. See Thomis (a); p. 11: Many in the middle classes in Nottingham had a working class background as the development of the textile industry had generated a certain degree of social mobility.

attempts of more thorough-going' reformers to 'take over'. The 'Corporation's political mission was as much to avoid revolution as to achieve reform [...]'.[254]

Amongst the ruling classes positions on the issue of parliamentary reform were complex and opposing fractions were irreconcilable. Even for the Whigs in Westminster, the party[255] which was to push forward the issue within the parliamentary system, parliamentary reform was a major source of dissent for many years. The party consisted of a rather uneasy coalition of aristocrats and professional men, with the former tending to call the tune, controlling a considerable number of seats in the Commons.[256]

In 1830 a new government was led by Earl Grey, who was as much a 'thoroughbred aristocrat' as the rest of his cabinet and had little sympathy for the developing workers' movement.[257] However it was Grey's administration that introduced a moderate Reform Bill. Debates began in the Commons on the 31st March 1831.[258] Although proposing an arguably minor extension of the franchise, the bill's core lay in the reorganisation of constituencies. The latter aimed at disfranchising many 'rotten boroughs' whilst others were to be reduced to sending only one MP to the Commons. A number of these seats were to be allocated to new constituencies, thereby strengthening parliamentary representation of the industrialising centres. The franchise in the counties was to remain with the 40s freeholders; in the boroughs it was to be held by all occupiers of buildings with an annual value of £10.[259]

---

254 Ibid; pp. 142/231.

255 See Wright; pp. 1-10: There were no political parties in Commons and Lords in the modern sense: 'the terms "Whig" and "Tory" were used, but normally only of the front bench professional politicians, those who were organised in small groups based on friendship, blood or marriage ties [...] or a rather vague sharing of attitudes. [...] "professional" politicians accounted for only one section of the House. There were also between a hundred and two hundred [...] "King's Friends" [who usually supported the government]. Their numbers included court officers, civil servants, government contractors, army and naval officers, [etc.] and sinecures and those sitting for government boroughs. Finally there were the mass of independent members who formed a majority of the eighteenth-century House of Commons. Some were lawyers and merchants, but most were country gentlemen [and] tended to support the government.'

256 Dinwiddy; pp. 1-5.

257 Wright; pp. 31. See Pearce; p. 67: '[...] back in 1812 the death penalty had been introduced for the destruction of machinery, [a piece of legislation which] would operate vigorously under the reforming Lord Grey.'

258 Goldsmith; pp. 470-1.

259 Wright; pp. 33-6. See ibid; p. 39: In the second Reform Bill the rules for the franchise in the boroughs were changed meaning that e.g. resident freemen were to retain their votes.

Why Grey's government pushed for parliamentary reform has been debated at length, for instance discussing whether hope for political gain or fear of revolution had been the government's primary motivation for pushing their Reform Bill.[260]

For Hernon, the popular movements' activities outside parliament, whose 'often uttered call [for reform] had become too loud to ignore any longer' was forcing the proposal of a bill.[261] In this interpretation, Grey sought a way to avoid revolution as it had occurred on the continent, a way which reacted to the on-going economic and social upheaval without endangering the established social hierarchies. This interpretation sees the Whigs' recipe to avoid revolution in 'granting concessions' whilst they were 'terrified' of the possible repercussions if they should fail.[262]

Following a different approach, Dinwiddy argues that 'although the state of feeling in the country was a major factor in [the Whigs'] deliberations throughout the Reform Bill Crisis, at no stage did it force them into anything like a capitulation'. He focuses on the political advantages the Whigs were hoping to gain by proposing their version of parliamentary reform, knowing that the issue would enjoy much public support.[263] This interpretation can be supported by arguing that bold claims like Goldsmith's, that the bill included 'a greater amount of change than had been anticipated either by friends or enemies',[264] greatly overemphasise the consequences of this piece of legislation. The carefully measured extension of the franchise and in particular the reorganisation of the constituencies aimed not at widening public participation in parliamentary politics, but at broadening the basis of the Whigs' political power. The pre-1832

---

260 Dinwiddy; p. 50-1.

261 Hernon; p. 58. See Dinwiddy; p. 46; Rudé; p. 88: There were a number of events which can be referred to in support of this interpretation, e.g. the Swing riots and the July Revolution in Paris. See Pearce; p. 156: 1831 saw a number of riots in Britain before the second bill was rejected in October, e.g. in Cyfarthfa where the military killed twenty persons. See Thompson; pp. 887-1: Thompson stated that the Reform Bill Crisis was not the consequence of 'a growing middle-class reform movement, with a working class-tail' pushing against the 'old corruption', but rather the 'agitation arose' from 'the people', forcing the middle-class to go along as they were the ones who could achieve a 'line of retreat acceptable to all', i.e. a compromise which would keep the working classes at bay whilst being tolerable to all but characters like Newcastle. However, this does not reflect the complex divisions within what can be constructed as working, middle and ruling classes.

262 Wright; pp. 31-3. See Pearce; p. 186: During the debates in the Lords, both sides saw the 'social fabric' endangered. For the Tories this danger originated 'from that unreliable thing [...] the people' whilst the Whigs stated that they were 'a reasonable bunch, providing the Lords did not enrage them by pushing their luck with a veto.'

263 Dinwiddy; p. 55.

264 Goldsmith; p. 471.

organisation of constituencies had given the Tories an advantage, as the majority of the 'rotten boroughs' were dominated by them. Therefore an attack on the 'rotten boroughs' would result in a major shift in the balance of power within the House of Commons. It is also noteworthy that plans to abolish a number of 'rotten boroughs' and to increase the number of county members were not designed to undermine the 'essential control of the system by the landed aristocracy and gentry', but to stabilise it. This was attempted by 'strengthening the legitimate influence of the landed classes over elections and a corresponding reduction of influences whose legitimacy was questionable.'[265]

The proponents of this very moderate parliamentary reform were faced with formidable opposition, not least by those within the ruling classes who were to lose power by the disfranchisement of many 'rotten boroughs'. One of most outspoken opponents of the Reform Bill was one of the most despised characters in Nottingham's history, the embodiment of all the clichés of the landed aristocrat,[266] Henry Fiennes Pelham Clinton, the Fourth Duke of Newcastle.[267] He was an 'ultra-Tory' of whom even Wellington said 'there never was such a fool'. Newcastle himself took pride in saying that he caused a riot wherever he went.[268] Economically and politically he was largely unsuccessful with most of his schemes and after

[265] Dinwiddy; p. 49-51; Wright; pp. 33-6. See Pearce; p. 98: Among the arguments brought forward against the Reform Bill was the fear that any reform would result in future demands: '[...] others will outbid you, not now, but at no remote period – They will offer votes and power to a million of men, will quote your precedent for the concession and will carry your principles for to their [...] natural consequence.'

[266] Gaunt (a); p. xi: 'In spite of owning property in Yorkshire, London and Wales, Newcastle was at heart a country gentleman and landed magnate who spent the majority of his time and energies upon projects associated with his wide ranging Nottinghamshire interests.'

[267] See Pearce; p. 202: '[Newcastle] was a character out of a melodrama, ready probably to water the workers' beer and happy to meet Reform by evicting tenants known to support it with the words "May I not do what I will with mine own?"'

[268] Bryson; p. 94; Thomis/Preston/Wigley; pp. 85-6. See Thomis (a); p. 149: Newcastle's reactionary views were so extreme as to enable even the Nottingham Whigs as to appear as 'popular egalitarians'. See Gaunt (a); pp. 74-5: An example for Newcastle's character is an event in January 1831. Whilst on his way to a ball in Newark, he was told that a 'large mob' waited for him and was 'insulting Every body that came up thinking that [he] might be in the carriage'. He continued to Newark, determined to rather 'Encounter any degree of riot than to incur the disgrace of retreat & to give to give the rabble a triumph'. On arrival he managed to get through some scuffles uninjured, satisfied that 'if I had not persevered in coming to the Town that I Should have Sacrificed my reputation & done irreparable mischief by giving courage to a set of miscreants'.

1830 he was constantly trying to avoid bankruptcy.[269] He was not an opponent, but an enemy of the Whig's Reform Bill,[270] not only as a matter of principle, but among the constituencies lined up to be disenfranchised were also some of 'his' own, among them all of his seats in Yorkshire.[271]

At first Newcastle had no need to worry, as the first Reform Bill was defeated in the House of Commons after seven nights of debate. However, Grey's defeat was followed by a general election in April and May 1831 which went badly for the opponents of reform, who lost numerous MPs, thereby securing future attempts for parliamentary reform a majority in the Commons.[272] In Nottingham both reform candidates were elected[273] and even Newcastle, used to obedient voters, was largely unsuccessful with his candidates. As even Newark failed to return a Newcastle family representative for the first time[274] the furious Duke wrote in his diary: 'I shall raise my rents to the double & see how they like that'.[275]

Following the elections, a second Reform Bill passed the Commons with a solid majority and was officially sent to the Lords on the 22nd September 1831.[276] In Nottingham 12,000-13,000 persons signed a petition in support of the Reform Bill, which was presented in the Lords alongside many other pro- and a few anti-reform petitions.[277]

---

269 Welch (a); pp. 1-2.

270 Gaunt (a); p. 77: 'I alone remain fixed in my determination & have to fight the cause almost single handed' whilst the other 'gentlemen of the County' driven by 'by fears or otherwise' are 'ingulphing [the] cause of reform'. See ibid; pp. 80-1: For Newcastle, parliamentary reform was aiming 'to overthrow the Nation'.

271 Ibid; p. xlii. See Welch (a); p. 1: Newcastle controlled several MPs: 'Before 1832 he had five M.P.s whom he nominated, two for Boroughbridge, two for Aldborough [...] and one for Newark. In 1830 he had seven candidates.'

272 Gaunt (a); p. xlii; Goldsmith; p. 472.

273 Field; p. 397.

274 Gaunt (a); p. xlii. See ibid; pp. 78-9: Newcastle's candidate in Newark, a Sir Griesley 'was very ill received & very roughly handled [...] there was so great a riot that he induced to retire [...] until [...] the Mayor had sworn in special Constables'.

275 Gaunt (a); pp. 80-2: Newcastle's electoral defeats in Nottinghamshire lead him to conclude that 'The county is carried by [...] revolutionists [...] not one man in it worthy of any distinction above the Swinish multitude'.

276 Goldsmith; p. 472.

277 Bryson; p. 94; *Journal*; 15th October 1831; *Mercury*; 8th October 1831; Thomis (a); pp. 221-2: The number of signatories stated varies in different sources. Pro-reform petitions were a regular feature in the Reform Bill Crisis, repeatedly being signed by thousands of people. See *Review*; 30th September 1831: The relative failure of the anti-reform petition was subject of mockery by proponents of the Reform Bill: 'Some of the Tories, in an evil hour for their cause, have ventured to get up a hole and corner petition; [...] during [...] two days, up to four o'clock on Saturday afternoon it had received the amazing number of 20 signatures!!!' See Pearce; p. 122.

But on Saturday, October 8th, at six in the morning, the House of Lords rejected the Reform Bill with a majority of forty-one.[278] The defeat came not as much of a surprise, but according to the *Mercury* there had been 'very few that entertained the remotest idea the majority would be so large.' Notable was the position of the church as twenty-two Bishops voted against the Reform Bill.[279]

A month later 'their effigies were burned before the Guy at many November 5th bonfires' and during the riots in Bristol (see 2.5.) the cry 'Down with the churches and mend the roads with them' was heard.[280]

[278] Bryson; p. 94; Hernon; p. 58; Pearce; p. 198. See *Journal*; 8th October 1831: 'On the Lord Chancellor declaring the state of the numbers, no expression of feeling took place.' See *Mercury*; 15th October 1831: 'Millions of subjects require a restitution of their rights; the King is ready to restore them; but one hundred and ninety Peers withstand the just demand.' See Pearce; p. 200: Placards in London shop-fronts soon read: '199 against 22,000,000'.

[279] *Mercury*; 15th October 1831: The *Mercury* contradicts itself regarding the exact number of opposing bishops, stating once that there had been 21 but elsewhere giving the number of 22. Only two bishops voted for the Reform Bill.

[280] Welch (b); p. 5; Pearce; p. 205: Charles Davies, the man who allegedly uttered these words, was later hanged.

2. The Reform Riots

A detailed reconstruction of the events which occurred in Nottingham and the town's neighbourhood between Sunday morning and Tuesday evening is a complex undertaking. Although it has been possible to examine plenty of accounts of the riots, there is no record that describes events from a rioter's point of view. Furthermore all the examined accounts were authored by men and often those men were for example Magistrates and military officers, desperate to justify their actions against the allegations of misconduct raised by Newcastle and others. Alternative versions of the events were given by those who had been targeted by rioters and were in many cases much inclined to blame the military and town officials for failing to protect their property. Other accounts came from prosecutors who were trying to prove their cases, and by newspapers who were keen to defend their political line and, even more crucially, sell their papers. Every party had an interest to depict events according to their respective agenda. Furthermore, whereas some accounts were written just days after the events, whilst information was still being gathered, other accounts were given years later, long enough for opinions and hearsay to develop into what may have seemed like accurate memories.

Whereas no description of past events can be a comprehensive account of what actually occurred at the time, this problem is even greater with regards to an event as chaotic as a riot. Therefore it is neither claimed that the following deliberations are a full account of the Reform Riots in and around Nottingham, nor that they are free of errors.

News of Reform Bill's defeat in the House of Lords reached Nottingham during the annual Goose Fair,[281] on Saturday 8th October 1831 at 'about half-past eight o'clock' in the evening with the arrival of Pickford's van.[282] None of the used sources report any form of direct action during Saturday night, possibly as the bill's rejection was not 'generally known' before Sunday morning.[283]

2.1. Sunday

The examined accounts vary how events unfolded during the course of Sunday morning and afternoon. In the aftermath of the riots much criticism of the town officials' conduct focussed on whether they had misjudged the situation during the day.[284]

It is undisputed that on Sunday morning around 10am a 'coneonrae of people' witnessed the arrival of the mail coach at the Post Office in High

---

281 Gray; p. 34.
282 Fellows/Freeman; p. 51; Hicklin; p. 159; *Mercury*; 15th October 1831.
283 Nottingham Corporation; pp. 96/111.
284 See ibid; pp. 104-6. See also see 3.2.

Street, near the *White Lion* hotel. Some accounts also reported that a passenger on that coach 'said that in London they were beating to arms, which was received with cheers'.[285]

There are a number of versions as to what happened next. The statements by the town clerk Enfield and one of the senior constables on duty that day, a Mr Jackson, both given in 1833, suggest that throughout the day the atmosphere in the town was not 'in an extreme state of excitement'. Enfield described that people were 'walking about in lots, but there was no appearance of them coming to a riot' and that they were rather discussing the rejection of the bill.[286]

Jackson stated that there were 'many people' on the streets but added that this was not unusual:

> 'There were many about the public houses, waiting till they were opened, to hear the newspapers read. I have been several years a constable; there was nothing in the state of the town to impress upon my mind that there was likely to be a riot.'[287]

However, according to the *Mercury* and the *Date Book*, the latter apparently drawing primarily from the former's account of events, the situation escalated for the first time immediately after the arrival of the mail coach, when Hedderly's shop in Clumber Street became the first target of direct action. Apparently the druggist stood in front of his shop, watching the crowd as the mail coach arrived nearby.[288] The *Mercury* recounts rumours of Hedderly using 'some offensive word or gestures' towards the crowd before retreating into his shop, but:

> '[...] we cannot learn that anything of the kind in reality took place, but a multitude is very easily excited, and the report caused some of his upstairs windows to be broken, though this was done by mere youths.'[289]

From Clumber Street the disturbance spread into Pelham Street where 'about the same time [...] it became apparent that the irritation was

---

285 Field; p. 399; *Mercury*; 15th October 1831; Thomis/Preston/Wigley; p. 85.

286 Nottingham Corporation; pp. 106/111-2. See Welch (a); pp. 9-10: As the Nottingham Watch Committee was not founded until 1836, the constables were not part of a regular paid police force but unpaid persons, only 'on call'. See NeC 4998: Manson described the constable who was send to protect him and his house as 'the most inefficient [...] and shabby looking fellow I ever saw'.

287 Ibid; p. 111.

288 Field; p. 399; *Mercury*; 15th October 1831.

289 Ibid. See Nottingham Corporation; p. 117: In 1833 Hedderly was ready to swear that he did not 'shew any remarks of gratification, in consequence of the Reform Bill being thrown out'.

progressively gaining strength'[290] when a Dr. Manson was 'hooted at and abused' before a 'Brick Bat was thrown' at him, which 'struck his Servant'.[291]

Regarding these differing versions of events, it seems likely that neither is completely accurate. Hedderly's shop was targeted again that evening and it seems possible that most of the damage was done at that point. However, neither Enfield nor Jackson directly denied that there had been some fracas in that area following the arrival of the mail coach and they were under severe pressure to downplay events in order to justify their conduct.[292] It also has to be taken into account that a certain degree of pushing and shoving, mixed with a bit of heckling and the throwing of a few stones were anything but unusual in Nottingham. This makes Barker's, Jackson's and Enfield's account of events believable, as for them a number of small frays and a large number of people on the streets would probably not have counted as a riot. On the other hand, it would have been naive of them not to anticipate that things could change very quickly, especially after sunset.

Manson and Hedderly had every reason to view any group of people on the streets with suspicions verging on panic. Both were very well known for their opposition of the Reform Bill. Their names had been printed by the *Review* little more than a week after they had, along with other 'respectable inhabitants' signed a petition 'against some of the clauses of the Bill [...] in terms of respectful moderation'.[293] The *Review* had written that the signatories, 'gentlemen who have viewed the reform bill "with the utmost anxiety and alarm", will unquestionably thank us for making known their names to the world'.[294]

The bookseller Mr Wright, who was later targeted by the crowds, stated:

---

290 *Mercury*; 15th October 1831.

291 NeC 4998.

292 Nottingham Corporation; pp. 95/106/109: Manson had accused them of failing to offer protection 'to his person and property, when danger was threatened' and ignoring his 'information, that the peace of the town was likely to be disturbed'. Enfield and the mayor, a Mr Barker, had told Manson at around 3pm that events were merely 'the ebullition of party feeling at the Bill not being passed' and that they were 'perfectly convinced there will be no riot in Nottingham'. Manson later stated: 'The Magistrates, in trusting to their own judgement, have proved that I was right, and they were wrong; and in consequence [...] a lasting disgrace [has been brought] upon the town and neighbourhood.'

293 Hicklin; p. 159; *Mercury*; 15th October 1831. See NeC 4998: Manson expressed his fury about this in a letter to the mayor: 'I have no doubt that the present Mob clamour and violence against me has been excited by a Paragraph in Sutton's *Review*, the week before last, reflecting upon myself and others for having signed a Petition against what is commonly called "The Reform Bill" [...]. Mr Sutton must look to the consequences.' See Nottingham Corporation; p. 98: Manson also stated that they had not petitioned 'against reform, but the first Bill; and the points we petitioned for were granted in the second Bill.'

294 *Review*; 30th September 1831. See Appendix XI. for the full list.

> 'I felt apprehensive on the Sunday morning, having heard that Bemrose, a bookseller of Derby had had his house destroyed by the mob, for having committed the same crime that I had done, that of signing an anti-reform petition.'[295]

Wright allegedly overheard various persons saying things like 'I should not wonder if they do [...] the same here' and knew that any of the 'nineteen of us, whose names were published in the paper' were 'marked men' as 'every inhabitant of the town knew that men' had gone 'to public houses to read the nineteen names'.[296]

Whether there was direct action during the afternoon, as suggested by Hicklin's account that as 'the day went on, the violence [...] gathered strength',[297] or not, as claimed by Enfield, Jackson and others; at 'the close of the afternoon' the crowd in the side streets of Clumber Street grew 'more dense' and stones were thrown at windows of 'obnoxious individuals.'[298]

> 'As soon as it became dusk, the individuals engaged in giving vent to their passions were flanked by several hundred young men and females who were drawn by the spot through curiosity, but whose presence greatly retarded the constables in their duty and the throwing of stones, brick-hats, &c. increased.'[299]

The rioting in the evening took place whilst Sunday's congregations were attending their gatherings. The parallel occurrence of rioting and worshipping gave Hicklin an opportunity to describe the wickedness of the rioters:

> '[...] as the song of praise, or the prayer of faith ascended from the worshipping congregations [...], the yells of an infuriated rabble, and the crash of broken windows, broke in with unwelcome sound on these sacred devotions, and told too fearfully that the work of devastation was commencing.'[300]

It seems that at around 7pm a crowd was indeed busy smashing windows at Hedderly's shop and soon other premises were targeted as well:[301]

---

295 Nottingham Corporation; p. 113.
296 Ibid; pp. 113-4.
297 Hicklin; p. 160. See Beckett (a); p. 119; *Review*; 30th September 1831: Hicklin was editor of the *Journal* and signatory of the anti-reform petition.
298 Fellows/Freeman; p. 51; *Mercury*; 15th October 1831; Nottingham Corporation; pp. 108/111-3; Wylly; p. 96.
299 *Mercury*; 15th October 1831.
300 Hicklin; p. 160.
301 Nottingham Corporation; p. 112.

'[...] when the congregations were leaving the different places of worship and the streets were much crowded, another party of rioters attacked in Bridlesmith Gate at Mr Ward's druggery store and then continued to the mentioned Dr Manson's house where they 'demolished a great many panes'.[302]

Manson later gave an account of the:

'[...] most tremendous attack [that] was made on my house by the mob; nearly the whole of the windows were broken [...] and every effort made by the Mob to break in at the door which was fortunately very strong and resisted their efforts to break it; large stone pieces [...] were thrown into the House that would have killed anyone struck by them.'[303]

As events escalated, the Mayor became the second known person wounded in the riots as he was hit 'on the head by a stone, thrown down and trampled on by the mob, his leg being much bruised'.[304]

The notorious Riot Act was being read and the constabulary tried in vain to repress the crowds:

'[...] the police officers exerted themselves to seize upon the offenders, but without avail, as it was utterly impossible to discover from what hands the stones were hurled, but each crash of the glass produced a loud shout, which was not unfrequently echoed by those who were idle spectators, yet who, in the excitement of the moment, gave way to the ebullition of their feelings.'[305]

Following these attacks, reportedly at about 8.30pm[306] a 'party of rioters' marched 'with loud cheers' towards the Market Square, where they made:

'[...] a determined attack upon the house of Mr. C.N. Wright, book-seller, Long-row. The mischief was principally done by the youths; but the moment [...] the constables attempted to

---

302 *Mercury*; 15th October 1831.

303 NeC 4998.

304 Beckett (a); p. 119; Fellows/Freeman; p. 51; *Mercury*; 15th October 1831; Wylly; p. 96. See Nottingham Corporation; p. 102-3/112: It is unclear when the mayor received the injuries to his leg and foot. According to Enfield and Jackson the mayor's head was hit by a stone at Hedderly's shop, after which he was 'so far incapacitated that he was obliged to be led away to the Police Office'. According to Enfield, trying to counter claims of town officials' incompetence by stating how valiantly they had behaved, the mayor tried again to 'disperse the people' whilst Wright's shop was being trashed and 'received a serious personal injury on the foot'.

305 *Mercury*; 15th October 1831.

306 Nottingham Corporation; p. 114.

> seize any of them, blows from stones and heavy hands plainly evinced that the lads were the mere instruments of more powerful agency. Not content with throwing in the upstairs of Mr. Wright, an attempt was made to break into the shop, in which they unfortunately succeeded; the front was completely battered in, and the books, prints, stationery &c. thrown about the street.'[307]

Crowds had apparently been able to defend themselves and were pretty much in control of the situation, having 'overpowered' the Mayor and constables. This only changed when the military arrived at the scene about half an hour later.[308] Commanding the local forces was Colonel Joseph Thackwell, in charge of the 15th Hussars, a cavalry unit stationed in Nottingham and Sheffield, which had been involved in the Peterloo massacre.[309]

Thackwell had received a first requisition for military intervention about midday, but not from the Magistrates and the Mayor of Nottingham but from those of Derby, where the riot was already in full swing. There the 'town was in the hands of a mob who were breaking windows and destroying the property of people who were obnoxious'. Thackwell responded by sending '44 soldiers and horses'.[310]

When the Hussars arrived, they were, according to the *Mercury*, 'received with cheers, and a great concourse commenced singing "God save the King"'.[311] The military started to disperse the crowds, though apparently without using excessive violence:

> 'The soldiers, with great caution and forbearance, proceeded to clear the street from the front of Mr. Hedderly's; but even their presence could not prevent the throwing of stones, and the smashing of the glass'.[312]

Following the arrival of the military, several prominent proponents of the Reform Bill attempted to calm the crowds:

> 'Mr. Alderman Oldknow earnestly exhorted the people to refrain from violence; and Mr. C. Wilkins got upon one of the stalls, in the Market-place, from which he addressed a large

---

307 *Mercury*; 15th October 1831.

308 Nottingham Corporation; p. 102/114.

309 Thomis/Preston/Wigley; p. 90; Wylly; pp. 94-5.

310 Fellows/Freeman; p. 51; Wylly; p. 95.

311 *Mercury*; 15th October 1831; Wylly; p. 96. See Beckett (a); p. 119: This is usually interpreted as evidence that the 'crowd saw their actions as [...] doing the king's will in demonstrating against a wicked faction'.

312 *Mercury*; 15th October 1831.

> multitude, and pointed out the folly of the excess; but his words, however much they might have convinced those who heard them, did not reach the persons who comprised what may be termed the mob, for they had hastily departed through different avenues at the first appearance of the military [...].'[313]

Thackwell stated that the military:

> '[...] succeeded in dispersing the crowds in various parts of the town and in the market-place. [...] Small knots of the lowest rabble, however, still continued to glide through dark alleys and passages, and frequently succeeded in breaking windows before they could be interrupted. [...] about 2 o'clock two of the rioters were apprehended [...] the streets were now nearly empty, the troops withdrawn to the barracks, an officer's piquet of 20 men being left in the town.'[314]

The *Mercury* lists the places that were targeted:

> '[...] in the course of the night, the houses of Mr. Bradshaw, wharfinger, Leen-side, Mr. Sharp, miller and baker, Mansfield-road, Mr. North, cheesemonger, Charlotte-street, Mr. Cooke grocery, Chapel-bar, Mr. Lowe, hosier, Pilcher-gate, and the Journal Office were visited and outrages committed.'[315]

According to Beckett, the 'atmosphere in the town on the Sunday evening was ugly, but not intimidating'. Events had not yet escalated beyond what had happened on so many other occasions when the people of Nottingham had engaged in direct action.[316]

2.2. Monday

Events on Monday started with a public meeting in the Market Square, which had been called by town officials after the rejection of the Reform Bill had become widely known on Sunday morning. This had been extensively

---

313 Ibid.

314 Wylly; p. 96. See Fellows/Freeman; p. 51; Nottingham Corporation; p. 102.

315 *Mercury*; 15th October 1831. See *Journal*; 15th October 1831: The *Journal* states that part of their office's front windows were destroyed, that food was expropriated from the houses of Sharp and North and that the house of the hosier Kewney was also attacked. Regarding the attack on their office the *Journal* later wrote: 'That we, as public journalists, should have incurred the displeasure of the populace, is more, we conceive, than our conduct has [...] warranted. Our desire has uniformly been to uphold the principles of good government [...] and to promote the best interests and welfare of all classes of the community.'

316 Beckett (a); pp. 119-20. See Nottingham Corporation; p. 97: According to Manson 'serious damage' had been done in the town.

publicised, as the local Whigs were 'anxious [...] to have a large meeting'.[317] The *Mercury* reports that 12,000 to 15,000 persons assembled 'with band and flags' and were addressed by various speakers.[318] It first seemed that Enfield's statement that everything would 'pass off peacefully' was correct. The crowd was very well behaved,[319] participating in what has since been described as 'a patriotic, not a revolutionary event' with people allegedly claiming to act 'on behalf of the king against the reactionary anti-reformers.'[320]

Among the noteworthy occurrences during that event was that a few 'young men' had:

> '[...] injudiciously, though without evil intentions on the spur of the moment, prevailed with the females to make a flag [of] a square of net, which was decorated with rosettes of black crape and bore the inscription "The Bill and no Lords"'.[321]

Being rarely mentioned in the accounts of the Reform Riots, women are in this instance depicted to have been actively involved, even though not acting autonomously but alongside men.

The *Mercury* claimed that towards the end of the meeting a rather mysterious stranger, who, according to the paper, had already addressed a smaller crowd which held a meeting in the Park, went up on one of the stages and addressed the crowd, 'displaying some strange gestures'. The meeting broke up with the band playing 'God save the King', after the assembly had 'been exhorted to peace and quietness'.[322]

Despite town officials' confidence that no further riots would break out, the 'whole constabulary force' of one hundred persons had been 'put on duty' and the troops were on high alert in their barracks, armed with firearms and swords, whilst a small military detachment was already in town. Beside Thackwell's Hussars and the constables a troop of Yeomanry

---

317 Ibid; p. 96.

318 *Mercury*; 15th October 1831. See Fellows/Freeman; p. 52: 'Leading liberals' spoke at the event: 'W.F.N. Norton, Esq.; Colonel Wildman; Lord Rancliffe; Thomas Wakefield, Esq.; Alderman Oldknow; Thomas Close, Esq.; Dr. Pigot, etc., addressed the populace and urged them to be quiet and keep the peace.' See *Journal*; 15th October 1831: Other speakers were Mr. T. Bailey, Mr. Hepner [...], Mr. W.P. Smith and a Mr C. Wilkins.

319 Wylly; p. 96.

320 Beckett (a); p. 121.

321 *Mercury*; 15th October 1831: The banner was 'carried through town', but seized by another crowd coming from the Park. When the 'Radford young men' complained to constables on Market Place, one of the Hussars seized the banner from the second crowd which had been moving towards Hockley.

322 Hicklin; p. 161; *Mercury*; 15th October 1831.

was stationed near Wollaton, commanded by a Major Rolleston. There were 'ominous signs for an outbreak occurring, [for instance] that the shopkeepers took the precaution of closing their shops, and all business was suspended.' Allegedly it was also 'quite evident, from the stern and fierce demeanour of many in crowd, that deadly mischief was contemplated.'[323]

The pro-reform *Mercury* was however careful to differentiate the crowd into 'those who may really be termed the men of Nottingham', i.e. those who listened to the speakers' pleas to behave with 'peace and quietness' and:

> '[...] an organized gang [...] ripe for every mischief. This gang consisted of all the low and bad characters in this neighbourhood – the pickpockets who were exerting their talents during the fair, and the vile and worthless of every description, who had come to the town under the hope of picking up some plunder at the races.'[324]

As the meeting came to an end it still appeared that the military would not be called upon to crush any disturbances that day. At half past two the town clerk reassured them that everything was calm, that people were going home and that the troops could stand down. But 'within the hour' the situation escalated as between 3pm and 4pm Mayor and Magistrates requested military support.[325]

By that time the 'lawless rabble'[326] had resumed 'the hunt for anti-reformers'[327] and already carried out a successful attack on a corn mill situated on the Forest,[328] belonging to a Mr Sharp, also a signatory of the anti-reform petition.[329] The mill got quite effectively damaged, its sails 'cut to pieces' and flour and corn 'scattered'. The mill's 'total demolition' was only prevented by 'a party of Hussars'.[330]

Following the attack on Sharp's mill, the Riot Act was read 'in many places' as 'mobs were parading through the streets with flags and doing

---

323 Fellows/Freeman; pp. 51-2; Hicklin; p. 161; Nottingham Corporation; p. 103/105; Wylly; p. 96.

324 *Mercury*; 15th October 1831.

325 Wylly; pp. 96-7.

326 Hicklin; p. 161.

327 Beckett (a); p. 121.

328 Fellows/Freeman; p. 52. See *Mercury*; 15th October 1831: By that time some windows in Hockley had already been demolished, belonging to the shop of Mr. Smith, baker and Mr. Prickard, grocer.

329 See *Review*; 30th September 1831. See Nottingham Corporation; p. 103: Enfield later stated that the attack on Sharp's mill had occurred on Sunday night.

330 *Mercury*; 15th October 1831: '[...] it certainly was a curious sight to see a number of little rogues of sweeps, who presented the most piebald appearance, from being plastered with flour.'

much injury to private property'.[331] Crowds were frequently attacked and dispersed. However, the seventy-five 'men and horses' under Thackwell's command were unable to control them.[332]

Some rioters armed themselves with 'bludgeons and iron palisades', torn up as they marched through Sneinton, and advanced 'after sundry minor depredations' onto Colwick Hall.[333]

The mansion was the home of John Musters, a Magistrate 'well known for his strict enforcement of the Game Laws'.[334] He has been described as 'an arch Tory who waged a vendetta equally against radicals and poachers' and was a 'well-known opponent' of the Reform Bill. Musters himself was not present at Colwick Hall at the time of the attack, but there were several of his servants, members of his family and at least one visitor. His son suffered a minor injury and his wife and other members of the household ended up crouching terrified under some shrubbery whilst Colwick Hall was thoroughly trashed and almost burned down.[335] However, no one in the crowd, which was later estimated to have been about 1,000 strong, seriously harmed anyone in the attack. Loseby, a servant sent towards town to inform the military of the attack, was stopped by the crowd who left him unharmed.[336]

Returning from Colwick the crowd was allegedly:

> '[...] uttering yells of frantic glee [expressing] the destructive intentions with which, under pretence of maintaining "the rights of the people" these misguided men had assembled.

---

331 Wylly; p. 97. See *Mercury*; 15th October 1831: 'The windows of Mr. Peter Loveitt, in York-street; of Mr. Clifton, an officer on half-pay, on the Mansfield-road; Mr. Tho[ma]s Berry, constable, Chesterfield-street; and Mr. Webster, constable, Derby-road, were broken, and considerable injury done.' See *Journal*; 15th October 1831: At Berry's house the doors were 'forced in, windows demolished, and furniture partly damaged'.

332 Wylly; p. 97.

333 Fellows/Freeman; p. 161.

334 Thomis (a); p. 226; Thomis/Preston/Wigley; p. 85.

335 Bryson; p. 95; *Journal*; 15th October 1831; 14th January 1832. See Hicklin; p. 161: 'Mrs. Musters, who was then in ill health, eluded the fury of the mob by escaping with her attendant to an adjoining shrubbery, where [she] lay concealed amidst the foliage till the hour of danger was past.' See *Journal*; 15th October 1831: 'The furniture in most of the rooms, including some of the most costly description, together with some valuable paintings, entirely destroyed, and jewellery of considerable value, with some plate carried off.' See also *Mercury*; 15th October 1831: Ale and wine were also seized and promptly consumed. See Appendix VI. for the full statement of Musters' son as reported in the *Journal*.

336 *Journal*; 14th January 1832: Loseby was pulled off his pony amid shouts of 'Pull him off, he is going for the soldiers' and 'Don't hurt him.'

> Having halted for the purpose of a little deliberation, a cry "to the Castle" soon announced the next object of attack.'[337]

Thackwell wrote that from about 7.30pm 'attacks were almost simultaneously [made] on the House of Correction and Nottingham Castle'. Bryson describes the attack on the House of Correction as a feint to divert the military, with the 'main body' of rioters splitting up 'to deal with the castle'. The evidence is however inconclusive as to whether the attacks were coordinated. In any case, it forced Magistrates, constables and military, including Thackwell himself, who had been 'out in the lower part of the town with a considerable part of [his] force', not to rush towards the castle, but towards the House of Correction. Crowds had been trying to 'force in the prison doors', but were soon repelled 'into the surrounding streets and alleys'. Thackwell then divided his forces, distributing dismounted soldiers 'for the protection of [the prison], the town and the county gaol, and the gasworks.'[338]

Although several hundred special constables had been sworn in prior to the attack on Colwick Hall,[339] the *Date Book's* description that they were preserving 'much private property from plunder' indicates that the priorities of these 'respectable people' were not the protection of the empty edifice of the detested Duke of Newcastle.[340]

Therefore the attack on the castle was undisturbed. It began as people extinguished all gas lamps between St. James' Church and the Riding School, indicating their practical experience in direct action. The 'two or three servants of the Duke of Newcastle' inside the Gate House, though being promised safety, refused to open the gates,[341] so the crowd tried to force them in. The gates first withstood the attack until a panel gave way. Three people slipped through, aiming to unbar the gates, while another

---

337 Hicklin; p. 162. See *Mercury*; 15th October 1831: 'Flushed with success, and full of desperate purposes, [the crowd was] uttering those wild shouts which, when heard through the stillness of evening and during a period of excitement, have the most appalling effect.'

338 Bryson; p. 95; Fellows/Freeman; pp. 97-8; Nottingham Corporation; pp. 103-4. See ibid: Enfield stated that '[...] when information was brought [...], that [...] the cry was, "to the Castle!" [...] there was a small portion of the cavalry mounted before the Police Office door. It was at that moment determined to take the remnant of the cavalry towards the Castle, [...] when a messenger came [...] with accounts that the mob were battering the gates of the prison, and that further force must be immediately sent to them. [A] cry [was] made, that the soldiers must go to the prison; and that was the way in which the step intended to be taken for the preservation of the Castle was prevented.'

339 Ibid; p. 105.

340 Field; p. 401.

341 Hicklin; p. 162/172. See ibid; p. 8 (appendix): Three persons were inside the Gate House at the time, the keeper, his wife and his brother.

party made a breach in the wall 'opposite to the steps leading to Standard Hill', enabling the rioters to storm the castle.[342]

> '[Having] forced their way past the lodge, [the crowd] poured in [the building] through a broken window, smashed the doors, and set about making a vast bonfire of this hated, if deserted, symbol.'[343]

Eventually, about sixty people entered the building itself, smashing the rails of the staircases, shattering windows and ripping down chandeliers. Allegedly a group of 'a dozen ringleaders' then paused to discuss the best method of burning the place down. Eventually holes were hacked in the floors, filled with broken tables and banisters, and set alight.[344]

> '[A] little after seven o'clock in the evening, the wild shouts of the mob [...] proclaimed to the town the accomplishment of their diabolical outrage.[345]

While someone was selling souvenirs, apparently one yard of ripped tapestry for the (rather outrageous) price of 3s, others busied themselves with the demolition of objects in the premises. Busts were smashed and the equestrian statue of the first Duke pounded with a crowbar,[346] according to Hicklin the action of a 'scoundrel' and a sign of a 'spirit worthy of the barbarians of the darker ages'.[347]

> 'About nine o'clock, the spectacle was awfully grand, and viewed from whatever point, the conflagration presented an exhibition such as seldom witnessed. The grand outline of the building remained entire whilst immense volumes of flames poured forth at the windows [...]. Thousands of people thronged the Castle-yard and every spot that commanded a sight of the fire. [...] The rain fell heavily, and the sparks came down in amazing quantities, so as literally to fall in showers. A stable or outbuilding [...] was also consumed.'[348]

---

342 *Mercury*; 15th October 1831; Hicklin; pp. 162/175: Grand entries are in reality often spoiled. Apparently someone fell into a well whilst storming the castle and had to be helped out 'by means if a long pole'. See ibid; p. 18 (appendix): It has been suggested that 'about six hundred' people attacked the castle gates.

343 Bryson; p. 95.

344 Hicklin; p. 162.

345 Ibid; p. 163. In spite of the slight inconsistency of the stated times, it is safe to conclude that the castle was stormed and set alight between 7pm and 8pm.

346 Field; p. 402; See Bryson; p. 95. Apparently one of the horse's legs was cut off. One the riders' feet turned up in a London antique shop.

347 Hicklin; p. 164.

348 *Mercury*; 15th October 1831.

As a 'consequence of [the attack on the prison] the troops [...] did not return to the market-place for some time, and when they did the castle was in flames.' Some soldiers and Magistrates eventually showed up at the castle yard but they did not try to disperse the crowds as 'there was but little chance of discovering the authors of the mischief among the great concourse of spectators.' Thackwell later admitted that military and Magistrates had not been in control of the situation during the night to Tuesday and concluded that it was not due to his few soldiers' presence but rather to 'the extreme wetness of the night that more mischief was not attempted'.[349]

During the night to Tuesday all efforts were made to reinforce Thackwell's small detachment of soldiers and the few constables. A 'great number of special constables were sworn in'[350] and the mustering of the South Nottinghamshire Yeomanry commenced, with many:

> '[...] troopers [having] a long and lonely [ride towards Nottingham] and not without risk for solitary yeomen, as the whole countryside was in a state of excitement.'[351]

2.3. Tuesday

The *Journal* wrote that in the morning the:

> '[...] outer walls of [the] once splendid edifice are alone left standing, and we fear will remain an eternal monument of the fury of a misguided multitude.'[352]

Nottingham Castle had become nothing more than a 'charred hulk'. Sadly, the bodies of two children were found, who had probably died exploring the smouldering ruins.[353]

---

349 Wylly; p. 98. See *Mercury*; 15th October 1831; *Journal*; 15th October 1831: Only the windows of a Mr Swann were broken. See Nottingham Corporation; p. 105: Apparently '10-12 prisoners' were taken that night, but nobody prosecuted, on 'account of the doubt of success in the prosecution'.

350 Fellows/Freeman; p. 51; Wylly; p. 98; *Journal*; 15th October 1831: According to latter 'to the number of one or two thousand.'

351 Fellows/Freeman; p. 53: They state that 'many of the yeomen were reformers, but that was not allowed to interfere with duty, and so in the rainy and dark night they rode hard to obey the summons.'

352 *Journal*; 15th October 1831; Bryson; p. 95. See Gaunt (a); p. 83; NeC 4999; NeC 5000: On Tuesday Newcastle, whilst still in London, was informed about the destruction of the castle and fears of an imminent attack on Clumber. In a rather panicked diary entry he expressed his hopes 'that Clumber is not in their black books' as he had heard rumours of 'many large houses' being destroyed. He concluded that the 'Whole country is in a horrid & fearful state'.

353 *Mercury*; 15th October 1831: The two children were S.S.N. Ellerby and Kilbourn. See *Journal*; 15th October 1831: They were six and eleven years old.

Again numerous people assembled at the castle where they were attacked by eighteen constables, five soldiers and one officer.[354] The soldiers engaged the crowd with drawn swords, using 'the flat sides of their swords to drive the most riotous back; in one or two instances the points were used, but without giving any but very slight wounds.'[355] Apparently it was then that for the first time during the Reform Riots people actively resisted soldiers by throwing stones at them.[356]

Coming from the barracks to reinforce the troops at the castle with a further twenty soldiers, Thackwell encountered a 'very large mob on the Derby road opposite the park, and these men being in the act of pulling down some iron rails, I rode among them and dispersed them'.[357]

In the early afternoon Hussars and Yeomanry repeatedly dispersed crowds all over town. Thackwell hurried towards Beeston after he had been informed that the crowd he had encountered on Derby Road had reassembled there.[358] On their way the people had stopped at the residences of four families to expropriate food and money, three of which belonged to anti-reformers, Col. Charlton, John Wright and Dr. John Storner. One was owned by pro-reform Whig Matthew Needham, whose house was apparently mistaken to be the home of said John Wright.[359] On their way they also visited some pubs where, according to Landlord William Martin of the Greyhound, some 'paid for their ale, and some did not.'[360]

---

354 NeC 5000; Wylly; pp. 98-9: Both sources contradict each other with regards to the party who dispersed the crowd. According to Thackwell it comprised of eighteen soldiers and one officer, according to Gell's letter to Newcastle there were mainly constables present, alongside a smaller band of soldiers.

355 *Mercury*; 15th October 1831. It is unsure whether the soldiers attacked the crowd with their swords before people started hurling stones. It can be speculated that the situation escalated as the soldiers were using their weapons, possibly ordered to do so after the mustering of special constables and Yeomanry had changed the balance of power in their favour. In any case, the confrontation set the tone of things to come.

356 Wylly; pp. 98-9: Until then Thackwell had found it 'worthy of remark, that whenever the military came in contact with the populace, the latter being dispersed did not offer the slightest resistance by throwing stones or otherwise.'

357 *Journal*; 14th January 1832; Wylly; p. 99: 'I had nearly twenty of the cavalry with me. Without making any charge I rode amongst them to disperse them. [...] Several of the mob told me I was acting illegally.'

358 Wylly; p. 99.

359 Thomis/Preston/Wigley; p. 86: One of those families later expressed their fury that the Yeomanry stationed at Wollaton Hall did not interfere. See *Journal*; 15th October 1831: '[...] in some instances every morsel of food was cleared off by the mob.' See *Mercury*; 15th October 1831: It is unclear whether this happened before or after the attack on Lowe's mill.

360 *Journal*; 14th January 1832; *Mercury*; 15th October 1831.

Eventually a crowd, according to later accounts 2,000-3,000 strong, marched towards Beeston silk mill, in possession of Mr Lowe, another well-known Tory. The mill, the largest in the East Midlands outside Derbyshire, had been built in the mid-1820s with 'no expense spared'. The rioters, allegedly operating with almost military precision, systematically smashed it up before it was eventually burned down.[361]

The attack on the mill has been interpreted as a sign of the rioters' growing confidence. The major actions on the two previous days had taken place after nightfall, whereas Lowe's mill was burned in broad daylight. According to Preston this success encouraged rioters to attempt a 'suicidal' attack on Wollaton Hall, the residence of the Seventh Baron Middleton, another Tory known to oppose the Reform Bill.[362] Rioters attempted to storm the gates near the crossing of Derby and Beeston Roads:

> 'But every preparation had been made. Col. Hancock had garrisoned the Hall with a strong body of colliers, and several pieces of cannon, and the Wollaton Yeomanry were stationed near the entrance. The mob, however, attacked the gate, which was forced open; the yeomanry immediately charged, the gate was closed, and sixteen or seventeen prisoners were taken.'[363]

As the Yeomanry headed towards town with their prisoners, they were attacked near the:

> 'Sir John Borlase Warren [where] the rioters ensconced themselves behind a wall in Chimley's Close, from whence they threw stones and bricks at the Yeomanry as they approached, and several of them were much cut and bruised. The Yeomanry fired their pistols, but without effect, as the mob, as soon as they had thrown, covered themselves behind the wall. This skirmish occupied some time, and soon afterwards the Hussars guarded the prisoners into the town.'[364]

---

361 *Journal*; 14th January 1832; Thomis (a); p. 226; Thomis/Preston/Wigley; p. 86. See Gaunt (b); p. 28: Tallents visited the site in January 1832 and 'saw the ruins, [all burnt] and broken, the roof tumbled down, the rooms [full of] rubbish, bricks and half burnt beams.' See Field; p. 403: The damage for 'the building, engines and machinery' was estimated at £6,650, for the silk at £1,140.'

362 *Journal*; 14th January 1832; Thomis/Preston/Wigley; p. 92.

363 Fellows/Freeman; p. 54; *Mercury*; 15th October 1831: The Yeomanry charge left one woman 'dangerously hurt'. Wylly; p. 99: Thackwell only arrived after the attack had been repelled, meeting Major Rolleston 'near Lenton'. See NeC 5004: The force at the gates was commanded by a Captain Edge.

364 Wylly; p. 99. See Fellows/Freeman; p. 54: The fight ended when '[...] one of the soldiers blew the lock [of the gate] to pieces with his pistol, thus enabling the Yeomanry and Hussars to enter the field. The mob promptly fled [...].' It seems probable that this ambush was a deliberate attempt to liberate the prisoners.

There were a few more clashes[365] as the prisoners were taken towards the county gaol:

> 'On the way the party was frequently pelted with stones, and in turning into Bridlesmith gate several stones were thrown which struck some of the escort. A pistol shot was then fired which wounded two people, and this at once stopped the hostile proceedings of the mob, and from that moment they melted away, nor did they ever again make head in any part of the town. [...] the man wounded was [...] a person who could be proved, were it necessary, to have thrown stones at the time.'[366]

This is contradicted by other accounts, which indicate that the neither of those wounded had attacked the soldiers. The *Mercury* and *Journal* both state that the shooter was one of Thackwell's officers,[367] a fact he apparently tried to cover up in the aftermath of the riots.[368] The whole affair had the potential to cause much controversy as the person who was severely injured, a tailor named Thomas Auckland, was a veteran who had been wounded at Waterloo.[369] According to the *Date Book*, he 'was taken to the General Hospital, and after a long confinement, recovered.'[370]

One aspect of Thackwell's version of events was not disputed: his Hussars had demonstrated that from now on they were going to shoot to kill. Unlike in the skirmish at Chimley's Close, where the paramilitary Yeomanry had discharged their pistols at rioters who were well covered behind a wall, allegedly only to 'intimidate' them,[371] at Bridlesmith Gate an officer of a regular army unit had fired into the unprotected crowd.

> 'The knowledge of the man being shot, seems to have struck terror in the mob, for from that moment they felt convinced, that the military, whom they had been led to believe, would not offer them any injury, would be no longer trifled with, and that they would now act against them with energy.'[372]

---

365 Wylly; p. 99: At least once stones were hurled at a different troop of soldiers outside the town, but the rioters 'were quickly chased away and a prisoner taken in the act of throwing was lodged in the county gaol.' See NeC 5004: According to this account, the Hussars took not one but '2 or 3 prisoners' in this incident.

366 Thackwell; p. 99.

367 *Journal*; 15th October 1831; *Mercury*; 15th October 1831. See Appendix IX.

368 Ibid: The *Mercury* reported that the adjutant of the 15th Hussars came into their office and begged them not to report that an officer had fired the shot.

369 *Journal*; 15th October 1831; Wylly; p. 99.

370 Field; p. 404.

371 *Journal*; 15th October 1831; Wylly; p. 99.

372 *Journal*; 15th October 1831.

At 5pm, the Mayor proclaimed a curfew and 'yards and lanes leading into the market place were boarded up.'[373] Heavy patrols were put in place and a few more scuffles occurred. By 7pm the 'Market-place was as quiet as it generally is at midnight.'[374]

Thackwell concluded his account of the riots by writing that the:

> '[...] last appearance of an assemblage of people was about 12 o'clock at night near the river, and those were dispersed by an officer's party with a town magistrate at its head.'[375]

'That was the end',[376] despite the verbal defiance shown by some in this crowd who allegedly shouted:

> 'What's the use of dispersing, we may as well die where we are as to go home and be starved.'[377]

2.4. Wednesday and Thursday

According to the *Mercury* many rioters went to sleep in the fields and by Wednesday morning they 'were seen dragging their weary bodies listlessly along the different roads towards the villages.' That day the scenery in Nottingham was still dominated by patrols of special constables, Yeomanry and Hussars, but 'Business was resumed. The market was held as usual'. By Thursday the 'town was in perfect quietness.'[378]

2.5. Riots in other parts of the country

When the Nottingham riots started on Sunday, they were already in full swing in Derby, where they had begun during the night. At least two people were fatally shot and three others wounded as the city and county gaols were attacked. At the former, twenty-three persons were liberated after rioters used a 'cast-iron lamp post' as a battering ram; at the latter, gunfire repulsed the crowds. Also in Derby, rioters targeted a number of known opponents of parliamentary reform. As in Nottingham, the riots were only quelled after the mobilisation of auxiliary forces, i.e. special constables and yeomanry, reinforced the few constables and the small military detachment Thackwell had sent on Sunday. By Monday evening special constables,

---

373 Beckett (a); p. 129.

374 *Mercury*; 15th October 1831: There were reports that some of rioters were still moving through town, allegedly armed not only with bludgeons, iron railings and stones, but 'a few had pistols'. See Field; pp. 404-5 for a description of how the riots simply ran out of steam.

375 Wylly; p. 100.

376 Welch (b); p. 9.

377 *Mercury*; 15th October 1831: That these exact words were actually used seems rather unlikely, but they may exemplify the sentiments felt by many rioters that evening.

378 Ibid.

'consisting of the respectable inhabitants', patrolled the streets 'in great numbers'.[379]

Although an unknown passenger on the mail coach that arrived in Nottingham on Sunday morning allegedly proclaimed that an uprising in London had already begun, rioting in the capital did not start before Monday. Large crowds gathered near Hyde Park and attacked the estates of the Duke of Wellington and various Bishops. Constables violently clashed with the crowds in and around Hyde Park, whilst the Marquis of Londonderry, on his way to the House of Lords, was surrounded by up to 4,000 people who sent a 'shower of stones' against him. He was only saved by military intervention. The House of Commons had to be protected by police squads and a 'general fight [...] ensued'. The police were assisted by 'several respectable-looking men who used every endeavour to put the mob to the rout.' After dusk the heavy fighting continued as crowds attempted to storm two police stations. Wellington was apparently quite shaken by the events and wrote that a revolution could be imminent. He described that the 'lower orders of the people [were] rotten to the core' and although not 'bloodthirsty [...] desirous of plunder' and willing to 'annihilate all property' which would result in the starvation of the majority of them. Even though fighting in London was fierce, it was short lived. According to the *Journal* there were no riots but only a non-violent congregation on Wednesday, shouting slogans like 'Down with the boroughmongers, down with the Duke of Wellington [...]' and placards were displayed in some windows stating 'The King, liberty, and reform.'[380]

The most serious riots took place in Bristol, almost two weeks after the events in Nottingham. They were triggered on 29th October by the arrival of one of the most outspoken opponents to the Reform Bill in the Commons, a Sir Charles Wetherall, Recorder of Bristol. His carriage was attacked but he managed to retreat to a mansion house in Queen's Square. Constables trying to attack the crowds were surrounded, disarmed and beaten. The military engaged the crowd as the mansion was about to be stormed and set on fire, Wetherall already having escaped over the rooftops. Cavalry charged and killed one person, dispersing the rioters for the night. Next morning the primary target was the military itself, especially the 'hated' Light Dragoons, who were 'chased' through town, though not without them killing several people. In the evening, the Mansion House, the Excise Office, the Customs House and some other houses around Queen's Square were looted and burned. Two gaols were stormed and prisoners liberated, the

379 Gaunt (b); pp. 26-7: Hernon; p. 59; *Journal* 15th October 1831. See Gaunt (b); pp. 26-7: Tallents' diaries provide quite a detailed account of the 'state of turmoil' in Derby. He reports of the surgeon Henry Haden being killed by a stone-throw and how he himself was sworn in as a special constable.

380 Hernon; pp. 60-1; *Journal* 15th October 1831; Pearce; pp. 200-1.

city's gallows thrown into a ditch, tollbooths and the Bishop's Palace burned. During the fighting the police showed such extreme brutality that at one point troops tried to restrain them by threatening to ride them down. However, ultimately it was the military that brought the riots to a close. On Monday there were a number of brutal cavalry charges, leaving hundreds injured or dead. The number of casualties is unclear, but according to Hernon even the government acknowledged the figure to be around 100 whilst other sources claimed it to be as high as 500 persons. Around 100 houses owned by 'grandees' were destroyed. A Colonel Brereton was put on trial after he had hesitated for days to order attacks such as the ones ending the riots with a bloodbath. He shot himself during the hearing. Five persons were sentenced to death, four executed, a further 88 transported or imprisoned. During the fighting crowds in other towns, for example Bath, engaged in active solidarity with the rioters as people tried to stop Yeomanry reinforcements marching towards Bristol.[381]

Further fierce fighting occurred in Worcester, less serious riots for example in Leicester, Tiverton, Darlington, Yeovil, Blandford, Sherbone, Exeter[382], Chatham[383] and Loughborough.[384]

---

381 Hernon; pp. 61-8. See Pearce; p. 205-6: He states that the riots in Bristol were ended by 'reinforcements under new military men given carte blanche by Melbourne [who] finally put down the mob in a distinctly Cossack way [which was] much applauded in the London clubs.' Pearce also quotes a statement by Greville regarding the massacre: 'More punishment has been dealt out than generally known, and some hundreds were killed or severely wounded by the sabre. One body of dragoons pursued a rabble of colliers into the country, and covered the fields with bodies of wounded wretches, making a severe example of them.' See Rudé; p. 98: According to Rudé the massacre ending the Bristol riots resulted in a dozen deaths, 100 injuries and a further 180 persons were detained, 50 on capital charges.

382 Hernon; p. 59: At Darlington a Lord Tankerville, who had voted against the Reform Bill in the House of Lords, was ambushed in his carriage: 'A double line of men ranged along the main street hurled paving stones, glass bottles and other missiles which they had earlier gathered into small piles. His Lordship and other noble occupants of the carriage escaped serious injury, but they were badly shaken.'

383 Beckett (a); p. 114.

384 NeC 5001: 'Several Houses in Loughboro' have been destroyed'.

3. The aftermath

In the immediate aftermath of the riots, Nottingham was described to have been 'in a feverish state'. Newcastle arrived at his mansion in Clumber on Thursday 13th October, still expecting an attack by 'these rascals' who had already shown such 'diabolical villainy'. By then Clumber had been stripped bare of all valuables and heavily fortified.[385] By the next morning, four days after his castle had been torched, Newcastle had found his confidence again, as he had 'heard of no fresh aggressions'.[386]

However, for months to come the 'whole country [was] in a tremendous & fearful state'. The Mayor of Nottingham begged Newcastle not to come near the town and the Duke agreed as he was sure to be 'infallibly murdered' if he should do so. During the winter of 1831-2 the fear that Britain was 'on the Eve of a bloody revolution' was fuelled by rumours of people having armed themselves or trying to procure weapons,[387] even though in reality, at least in Nottinghamshire, there were only a few stack-fires.[388]

For Newcastle, the determined class warrior, the prospect of revolution was not as dreadful as many others in the middle and ruling classes. Instead, he:

> '[...] rejoiced that at last they see the necessity of making a Stand & to risk anything Sooner than yield to the dictation of

---

385 Gaunt (a); pp. 84-5: Newcastle was confident to repel '20,000 men' as 'the preparations are indeed formidable' with 70 Yeomanry cavalry and a further 200 heavily armed men at the house which was 'filled with men in all the rooms, with cannons, of which I have 10 3 pounders & 14 little ship guns & fire arms muskets & pistols & sabres planted in their proper positions & in all the windows'. See NeC 5010: Newcastle failed to mention that one person, the carpenter Joseph Bains, died after being shot accidentally in the ante room to the library.

386 Gaunt (a); p. 85: Newcastle reduced the number of armed men on the premises, no longer admitting any 'of them into the house'. He returned to his favourite method of passing time, decorating Clumber which he found to be 'Scarcely habitable [...] full of litter & dirt'. He was confident that he and his family 'shall soon be all together & comfortable again'.

387 Gaunt (a); pp. 87-8; Pearce; pp. 208-14; Thomis (a); pp. 231-2; Wylly; pp. 103-4: Such rumours circulated throughout the winter 1831-2. There were also rumours of plans to attack Thackwell's Hussars or to liberate the prisoners. A troop of artillery and further 150 soldiers were stationed in Nottingham. See Thomis/Preston/Wigley; p. 99: In December Major General Sir H. Bouverie issued the mayor of Nottingham with 100 muskets, 2,000 rounds and the Board of Ordnance issued bankers Samuel Smith and Co. with a supply of hand grenades.

388 Ibid; pp. 92-3. Nottingham Corporation; p. 38: An infantry regiment was still sent to the town.

> the Mob – The Spirit is now fast appearing in other parts of the Country – If it should become general, the revolutionists & anarchists will not long be able to make head against it'.[389]

However, his determination was never put to the test as revolution never came.[390]

3.1. Praise for the soldiers, the scaffold for the rioters

Although they also faced heavy criticism,[391] Thackwell and his Hussars, the constabulary, the Magistrates and the Yeomanry were highly praised for their conduct by superior officers and some 'gentlemen of the highest respectability in the town and county' as 'the late most formidable tumults were effectually suppressed and the public peace preserved without the loss of a single life and almost no bloodshed.'[392]

> 'The zeal, gallantry, and good temper with which they so promptly dispersed the rioters, and the patience with which they endured the fatigues of an arduous and harassing service, have obtained the unqualified approbation of Colonel Thackwell, of the King's Hussars, and the gratitude of the town and neighbourhood of Nottingham.'[393]

The local newspapers also gave the 'greatest praise' to the 15th Hussars:

> '[...] for the temper with which they have conducted themselves during this most trying period; constantly on duty for three nights and two days, they have uniformly behaved with firmness and moderation; and even when excellingly provoked, did not allow themselves to be irritated. We must also withhold the tribute of just approval from the police of the town, and the respectable inhabitants who have joined in guarding the property of themselves and neighbours.'[394]

Alongside the praise of those who quelled the riots went the persecution of alleged rioters.[395] It was later said that it had to be demonstrated:

---

389 Gaunt (a); p. 89.

390 Wright; pp. 47-8.

391 See 3.2.

392 Fellows/Freeman; pp. 56-7; Nottingham Corporation; p. 103; Wylly; pp. 100-3.

393 DD2069/1.

394 *Review*; 14th October 1831.

395 See Hicklin; p. 173: The Secretary of State issued a proclamation on the 18th October 1831 regarding the destruction of the castle, promising a pardon and a reward of £500 to anyone (except the 'person who actually set fire to the said property') who 'shall discover his accomplice or accomplices therein, so that he, she, or they may be apprehended and convicted thereof.' See *Journal*; 21st January 1832: Newcastle himself never offered a reward.

> '[...] that the law can never be violated with impunity by the few or the many – by the midnight assassin [...] or by the overwhelming thousands who hope to escape on account of their numbers, or a dense crowd.'[396]

Knowing that the prosecutions would be unpopular, it was tried to depict the actions of the rioters as a danger to all:

> 'I need not [...] to enter into the subject of the necessity of such crimes being checked, as they strike at the security of property, whether of the rich or the poor; and as they lay open to attack the cottage of the mechanic as well as the mansion of the rich; for if a lawless mob can with impunity thus destroy property, it is only necessary for a little mistake or delusion to occur, to render any place the object of destruction.'[397]

Some of the prisoners seized during the riots were speedily put on trial, for instance one person who had thrown stones at a troop of soldiers after the fight near Wollaton Hall. On Monday 17th October he was found guilty and sentenced to one year in prison.[398]

In the three months leading up to the main trials, the local Magistrates were trying to 'keep excitement down' by using 'clandestine' investigations, which basically meant secretly arranged arrests and repeated attempts to thwart the accused from making adequate preparations for their defence.[399]

In January 1832 the imprisoned people were to be put on trial before a Commission of the Special Assize under a Sir Joseph Littledale and a Sir Stephen Gaselee.[400] On 4th January 1832 the Special Assize opened at Shire Hall:

> 'Every precaution had been taken, as well to preserve the public peace, as to prevent any insult being offered to the bearers of his Majesty's Commission, and a large body of

---

396 Ibid.

397 Ibid.

398 Fellows/Freeman; pp. 57-8: The person's trial was held at the County Quarter Sessions. He was found guilty of 'assembling with divers other persons unknown, in the parish of Radford, [...] and then and there committing a breach of the peace by throwing stones at the Yeomanry Cavalry.' In addition to his prison sentence he had 'to enter into his own recognizances of £30 and two sureties of £10 each to keep the peace for twelve months, in default of finding securities to six months further imprisonment.'

399 Thomis (a); p. 233. *Journal*; 15th October 1831: According to the *Journal*, in the immediate aftermath of the riots 'Apprehensions of suspected characters are almost hourly taking place.'

400 Hicklin; p. 169.

> special constables [...] lined the way from the entrance into the town to the Hall [...]. Detachments of military on horse and foot, were also stationed in such directions, that a strong force could have been brought to action [...] in the course of a few minutes. All, however, we are happy to say, passed off quietly.'[401]

The Special Assize primarily occupied itself with four events:

> '[the] burning of Colwick Hall, and the demolition of property there; [...] the burning of Nottingham Castle; [...] the burning of Beeston Mill, and the destruction of property there; and [...] the riots at Wollaton.'[402]

Twenty-three persons were 'put on the bar' for their alleged actions during the Reform Riots, all facing capital punishment. Various others were tried for unrelated offences including theft and sexual violence.[403] Seventeen others, most of them prosecuted for the riot in Wollaton, were apparently acquitted without their cases being dealt with in detail.[404]

Trials regarding the burning of Lowe's mill[405] began on the third day of the Special Assize. The indicted was George Beck, a 20-year-old from Wollaton.[406] He was systematically depicted to have been a ringleader, commanding the crowd like a general his troops, carrying a 'tri-coloured flag', or, according to the constable who nicked Beck, 'a stick with some tri-coloured ribands on it'. The alleged military precision of the crowd was

---

401 *Journal*; 7th January 1832.

402 Ibid. See Appendix X. for a summary of the Special Assize's proceedings.

403 DDFSI/134; *Journal*; 7th January 1832; NeC 5052. For a (probably incomplete) list of those imprisoned for their alleged actions during the Reform Riots see Appendix II. See *Journal*; 7th; 14th; 21st January 1832: The *Journal* provides details regarding the trials against three persons (George Forman, Richard Branston and Thomas Grundy) who are not referred to in the document DDFSI/134. See NeC 5052: Forman and Branston had been discharged 'on Recognizance to appear when called on' and were therefore not on the 'Calendar of Prisoners'.

404 DDFSI/134: Six persons listed in the 'Calendar of Prisoners' and charged with offences connected to the Reform Riots were apparently acquitted without a trial: Aaron Booth, Elizabeth Hunt, Samuel Binks, Thomas Carlin the elder, Thomas Carlin the younger and William Green. See *Journal*; 14th January 1832: The 'Grand Jury [also] ignored the bill against James Bartle, W[illia]m. Scottoms, James Lowther, Samuel Horsley, W[illia]m. Butler Elliott, David Potts, John Allen, W. Armitage, Felix Testot, Thomas Allen, and Joseph Hind, who had all been out on bail, for the riot at Wollaton.'

405 Ibid; 7th; 14th; 21st January 1832; see Appendix X.: The Special Assize spend two days with the trials against those alleged to have attacked Lowe's mill, two days with the wrecking of Colwick Hall and one day with the destruction of Nottingham Castle and the repelled attack on Wollaton Hall.

406 DD763/8.

interpreted as an aggravating factor, as were the crowd's alleged brutal intentions which were referred to repeatedly by witnesses stating that rioters had looked for 'old Lowe' shouting 'Where is he? We will cut him to pieces and frizzle him.' Beck was found guilty.[407]

Over the following days, trials continued with a number of witnesses being questioned, among them discharged prisoners, constables, Yeomanry troopers and prominent targets of the rioters like the son of John Musters of Colwick Hall. Five more people, George Hearson, John Armstrong, Thomas Shelton, David Thurman and William Kitchen were declared guilty for their alleged involvement in the destruction of Lowe's mill. For their alleged actions at Colwick Hall the jury found Charles Berkins, Valentine Marshall and Thomas Whitaker to be guilty. Various others were acquitted, on the sixth day of the procedures five persons at once, a verdict which was 'received with loud cheers in the Hall.'[408]

Friday the 13th saw the trials against Joseph Shaw and Robert Cutts, both indicted for 'riotously and tumultuously assembling with others [...] and unlawfully and maliciously setting fire to Nottingham Castle'. Shaw was almost immediately acquitted. The case against Cutts was based on him having returned home with a 'dirty face' on the night the castle burned, and his alleged boasting to have lit 'three of six fires' there. Faced with the question whether these 'declarations were confessions of guilt, or [...] idle boast', even the prosecutor recommended to acquit the accused. The jury agreed and Cutts was released after Littledale told him that 'if the habits of your past life have been wicked, I exhort you immediately to amend them.' Cutts' acquittal meant that no one was convicted for the destruction of the castle.[409]

Statements given during the trials are the only accounts of the rioters themselves, or, to be precise, of persons charged with rioting. However, as

---

407 CHM 5/6; *Journal*; 14th January 1832: 'When the mob got to Beeston, the prisoner headed them, and on getting to the mill, he said "Halt, front, this is the place; fall round and do your duty." According to the testimony of witness William Turton the people in the crowd did act methodically and communicated with each other, e.g. to stop stones being thrown at the building whilst rioters were still inside it. Allegedly some in the crowd discharged pistols.

408 *Journal*; 7th; 14th; 21st January 1832. See Gaunt (b); pp. 29-30: Hearson had been able to bring 'six or seven witnesses to prove an alibi', but to no avail. Tallents repeatedly wrote of his frustration regarding the acquittals which he blamed on 'most horrible', 'infamous', or 'shocking' juries, which were 'evidently prejudiced in favour of the prisoners.'

409 Hicklin; pp. 169-77: 'It was [...] a well-ascertained fact, that although no conviction for burning the Castle took place, several of the prisoners, who were found guilty of other acts of incendiarism perpetrated during the riots, had also been concerned in the outrage at the Castle [...].'

the indicted were facing capital punishment, it is not surprising that they did not help their prosecutors by commenting on their actions and motivations, but rather gave statements like 'the mob laid hold of my arm, and linked me in'.[410]

The prosecution was using witnesses who had themselves been indicted but since discharged. Aaron Booth, a 19-year-old from Carlton, who had been 'confined in prison on charge of riot', testified against others after his acquittal.[411] Other witnesses gave evidence for economic reasons. Charles Slater, a fifteen or sixteen year old farm worker who was frequently without work and income, testified against a number of persons, including Beck, Hearson and Armstrong. He had been called an 'accomplice' of the rioters and claimed to have witnessed the attack on Lowe's mill. He had been taken 'before the Magistrates' by his father after he had seen 'bills offering a reward'.[412]

Out of the twenty-three persons against whom the Special Assize made detailed cases for offences related to the Reform Riots, fourteen were acquitted.[413] Of the nine persons who had been found guilty, four, David Thurman, William Kitchen, Valentine Marshall and Thomas Whitaker were 'recommended to King's mercy', i.e. they were 'to be transported for life':[414]

> 'His Lordship [...] said [...] they must not expect that they would have a small punishment. There is no doubt his Majesty will suffer them to remain in this country; they must therefore, prepare to leave it, and when they get into a foreign land, they will not have similar comforts to those they have here, but they will have a life of suffering and of privation.'[415]

George Beck, whom the jury had recommended 'to mercy, on the ground of his previous good character', was denied this by the judge who justified

---

410 *Journal*; 7th; 14th; 21st January 1832: A version of events that was frequently given by those indicted was that they went to see the ruins of the castle on Tuesday morning, from where they were sent away by soldiers. Eventually finding their way into the Market Place, they then set off towards Beeston and observed the direct action at Lowe's mill before being arrested, mostly by Yeomanry troopers.

411 Ibid; 14th January 1832: Without further evidence, the claim that Booth, a very young person charged with a capital offence, might have been coerced to agree to a deal allowing him to be discharged if he agreed to testify against others, is nothing but speculation but anything but impossible. See Gaunt (b); p. 29: Booth had been 'examined' by Tallents and his father on Sunday.

412 *Journal*; 14th January 1832.

413 Ibid; 7th; 14th; 21st January 1832: Some of the twenty-three were tried twice on different charges.

414 Gaunt (b); p. 30; *Journal*; 21st January 1832. See Beckett (b); p. 314: Marshall was lucky and eventually became a successful florist in Tasmania.

415 *Journal*; 21st January 1832.

his decision by highlighting Beck's alleged prominent role in the attack on Lowe's mill.[416]

He and the others not recommended to 'mercy' were told:

> '[...] that their lives were forfeited, and that they had but a short time to live; and that their fate would afford an example, that though a mob might triumph for a short time, the law would ultimately be too strong for them.'[417]

The 'general feeling in the town and neighbourhood was so averse to the execution of the sentences, that every possible appeal was made'.[418] A petition was drafted to the Commons stating that the prisoners had been given insufficient chances to prepare their defence and the Magistrates had resorted to threats and privations to force confessions. It was signed by 17,000 people, a similar petition to the king by 25,000.[419] The relatives of the 'condemned men at Nottingham' even approached Newcastle, begging him to sign the petition. He refused but noted in his diary that not the 'poor devils' but rather his political opponents in the Commons 'ought to suffer punishments' as the former had been 'Set on by' the latter.[420]

On the Saturday before the executions were scheduled, all of the convicted, with the exception of Shelton, desperate after the petitions seemed to have been in vain, attempted to escape. They never even made it out of their cell and were then put 'into double irons'.[421] The following day:

> '[...] the official order for their execution was received; and on Monday, their friends were admitted to take their last leave of them; the scene was [...] distressing, inasmuch as there was a large iron gate between the prisoners and their friends,– nor were the agonized parents permitted so much as to shake hands with their unfortunate children!'[422]

---

416 Idem; 14th; 21st January 1832. See Gaunt (b); p. 29: According to Tallents' the 'excessively dull' jury had given 'no sufficient grounds' to recommend Beck 'to mercy'.

417 CHM 5/6.

418 Field; p. 406.

419 Bryson; p. 96; Thomis (a); pp. 233-4; Welch (b); p. 10.

420 Gaunt (a); p. 93.

421 DD763/8; See Field; p. 406: Day after day, however, rolled by, but brought not the desired relief; and [...] though guarded by a strong military party [...], the men meditated an escape! During the afternoon of Friday, they expressed a wish to be alone [...]. Suspicions were however excited, and on examining one of their beds on Saturday evening, the blankets were found to be slit up and tied together [...]. With these they had intended to let themselves down into Narrow-marsh; but the design was frustrated, and those engaged in it heavily ironed.'

422 DD763/8.

Thomas Shelton and Charles Berkins were however lucky. On the day before the executions 'a respite during His Majesty's pleasure arrived', leaving them rejoicing and the others in despair, 'the last ray of hope [having been] shut out.'[423]

On Wednesday, 1st February 1832:

> '[The] die [was] cast! And nought remains for us but to lament their fate. [...] At an early hour this morning, the passage along the High-pavement was stopped by a numerous body of constables; the 15th Hussars, and the Queen's Bays, together with the 18th Foot, were also there to support the civil power, so formidable a force was never before assembled in Nottingham. At 20 minutes to twelve, the unhappy men were brought out [...] and many people called out "Murder." They were soon tied, the scaffold fell, and their earthly sufferings were terminated.'[424]

3.2. Newcastle's compensation

The trials of alleged rioters were not the only legal proceedings in the aftermath of the Reform Riots. The furious Duke of Newcastle blamed town officials for the destruction of his castle as well as the attack on Colwick Hall:

> 'It is perfectly clear that the Magistrates & authorities took not the slightest pains to prevent the infamous outrages at Colwick & Nott[ingha]m Castle, [...] the slackness in the performance

---

423 Ibid: Shelton's and Berkins' 'feelings of gratitude and thankfulness cannot be described. They were immediately removed from their unhappy companions, who now saw their doom was fixed [...].' It had been widely hoped that all executions could be prevented: 'Never, never can we be the apologists for arson and plunder, but we had fondly hoped that the Ministers of the Crown would have supposed that the justice of the ease would have been amply met, by sending the guilty parties to another country, without inflicting upon them the punishment of death [...].'

424 Ibid. See Field; p. 407 for a rather heart-breaking account of Hearson's final minutes: 'A friend offered Hearson his arm, which he refused, saying, "No, I will go by myself." He advanced at a quick pace, and on reaching the steps, notwithstanding his irons, ran quickly up, jumping upon the scaffold. He then took off his white cap from his head, and twirled it round in his hand, along with his black neckerchief, as if in triumph, while the multitude gave several loud cheers, and his feet moved as if he were dancing. [...] He was at length persuaded to desist from any further display, and he stood composed while the rope was adjusted. It was found necessary to pinion his arms tighter, and whilst the hangman was fastening the knot, he looked up and said, "Give me plenty of drop, and do not let me suffer much punishment." His eyes were then bound round with the neckerchief.'

> of their duty on all occasions [...] has been signally remarkable, they shall hear more of this.'[425]

Initially, he demanded an inquiry as he hoped 'that a public example will be made of those who have been Either criminally negligent, or nefariously collusive.'[426]

As Newcastle had been in London during the riots and avoided Nottingham in the immediate aftermath,[427] he had to rely on second-hand information. His suspicions towards the local authorities seemed to be confirmed by a number of reports. Notably was an anonymous letter, sent to him on October 19th, in which allegations were made that the soldiers had neglected their duties as they would have easily been able to defend Colwick Hall, Nottingham Castle and Lowe's mill. It was also stated that the Mayor had (at the very least) made a fatal error when he called the meeting in the Market Place on Monday morning. The anonymous writers' claim that both Colwick Hall and the castle had a guard of twenty soldiers each at the time of their destruction contradicts every other source and can therefore be dismissed with ample surety. The suggestion that the attack on Lowe's mill could probably have been thwarted by the soldiers stationed at Wollaton is not as weak, but will not be discussed further as the used sources do not provide enough information regarding the activities of the Yeomanry at Wollaton.[428]

Questions whether the direct action at Colwick Hall and the castle had been successful due to the inefficiency of troops and Magistrates, either because of their incompetence or as a result of deliberate inaction, have been brought forward in accounts by historians[429] as well as by the rioters' contemporaries.[430] Musters' wrote that his butler saw crowds in Sneinton marching towards Colwick and had tried to persuade Thackwell to send a

---

425 Gaunt (a); p. 86. See NeC 5021: Musters was similarly outraged by the alleged failings of Thackwell and the Magistrates. See NeC 5030: An anonymous letter blamed those in the castle lodge who: 'must have heard and seen the tumultuous manner the mob conducted themselves on Sunday evening and the next day [...]. They are not worthy to be trusted anymore.'

426 Gaunt (a); pp. 86-7: Within days he lost interest in an enquiry and wrote that it would be a 'dead letter in the hands of the magistrates themselves who of course will do nothing – It would be a mere mockery of enquiry'.

427 Wylly; pp. 94-5: Newcastle realised that he 'should do more harm than good by appearing at Nottingham; [as] my presence will [...] raise a mob.'

428 NeC 5026.

429 See Fellows/Freeman; pp. 55-6: They wrote that the 'Whig Magistrates and their friends [...] persisted in [...] inefficient courses'.

430 See NeC 5004; NeC 5016; NeC 5026; Nottingham Corporation; p. 97-8: Manson stated that the Magistrates had been 'inactive' and that 'proper steps [...] taken in the first instance [...] might have stopped the riots.

band of soldiers towards Musters' estate. Thackwell had apparently stated that he would have been happy to oblige if ordered to do so, but, for fear of exposing the town, the Mayor denied the request.[431] Thackwell did indeed never commit troops without being authorised to do so, something for which he was later criticised during the Special Assizes.[432] It is unclear whether Thackwell's inaction at this time was due to a strategic decision to keep his troops in Nottingham, or to the absence of a county Magistrate, i.e. a Magistrate whose jurisdiction covered Colwick Hall. In any case, it left Musters' estate 'to the mercy of the rioters'.[433]

A letter by Thomas Moore, the High Sheriff of Nottingham described events after the crowds had returned from Colwick:

> 'Hearing of the attack about to be made upon the Castle I immediately applied to the County Magistrates present for Troops to act against them, but I lament to say that they thought the force in the Town so weak that it would endanger the safety of the Town by dividing them [...].'[434]

Similar claims were made by Hicklin, who furthermore stated that 'the smallest band of soldiers might have saved the castle!'[435]

The decision not to send troops to defend the castle, even though it was such an obvious target, has led to speculation whether the Whig Magistrates of Nottingham took the opportunity to 'revenge themselves' on the despised Duke.[436] Although this may have very well been a factor, neither this claim nor the one that they did not care about the castle as it was extraterritorial, thereby relieving the town of the responsibility to pay compensation for any damage, does seem to be sufficient to explain their decision making process.

Thackwell simply argued that he did not command a sufficient force to suppress the riots before Tuesday. Apparently well aware of Newcastle's fury, he carefully drafted his report to the Duke, writing that 'the Mayor and

---

431 NeC 5021. See Wylly; p. 97: In Thackwell's report to Newcastle he justified this decision not to allow 'any part of the military to leave the town' because of the 'weakness of my force, and the alarming appearance of the multitude which filled the street.'

432 See NeC 5016; Thomis/Preston/Wigley; p. 90. See *Journal*; 14th January 1831: Judge Gaselee stated that private citizens and the military do not need to 'wait the order of a Magistrate [...] before they act'. See Nottingham Corporation; pp. 25-6: Apparently the jurisdiction of county Magistrates had been extended to cover both town and county, though Beckett's arguments suggest that town Magistrates could not operate in the county.

433 Beckett (a); pp. 124-5.

434 NeC 5004.

435 Hicklin; p. 165.

436 Bryson; p. 96.

the Magistrates exerted themselves to preserve the peace of the town, and afford assistance as far as their means would permit.'[437] The Magistrate Norton returned the favour in his own report to Newcastle, writing that:

> '[...] had there been at first a sufficient Military force at hand, I believe we could have saved the Castle [...]. I cannot conclude this communication without [...] representing to your Grace [...] the merits of Colonel Thackwell whose [...] ability with a very limited force appear to me entitled to the utmost praise.'[438]

Thackwell's and the Magistrates' decisions how to deploy their troops do indeed appear reasonable from their point of view. The weak military forces in the town had been overstretched all day, being reinforced at that time only by a few constables and a limited number of untrained special constables, the latter apparently more motivated to protect their own property than that of Newcastle.

It might well have been possible to dispatch a small detachment of troops to Colwick Hall whilst retaining the ability to repress direct action within the town, not least as a significant number of rioters had gone off to trash Musters' estate. But after the attack on Colwick Hall, an escalation which went well beyond the usual window breaking and constable bashing, Thackwell and the Magistrates were again confronted with the decision on how to distribute their forces.

It was up to them to uphold the laws of the propertied and they decided to send soldiers to the House of Correction and the town and county gaols, i.e. to defend institutions which did not only have a symbolic function, but very practically created class discipline by repression. Furthermore they chose to guard the gasworks,[439] a vital part of the town's infrastructure. It also made sense for Thackwell and the town's officials to keep the Yeomanry stationed at Wollaton. Seizing Colwick Hall had demonstrated the rioters' readiness to go the extra mile for a tempting target. Wollaton Hall was, like Colwick had been, a residence actually inhabited by a member of the ruling classes and filled with valuables, whereas the castle was little more than an abandoned shell. Apparently Thackwell and the Magistrates prioritised the wider interests of the middle and the ruling classes over the particular interests of one member of the ruling classes. In other words, they chose to defend instruments of power and repression, infrastructure and as much

---

437 Wylly; p. 98. See ibid; pp. 94-5: Newcastle had requested the 31st October Thackwell's 'impartial account' of the events.

438 NeC 5015. See *Mercury*; 15th October 1831: It is questionable how much faith Newcastle put into the words of someone who was not only one of the accused Magistrates but had also spoken at the rally on Monday morning.

439 Thomis/Preston/Wigley; p. 91; Wylly; pp. 97-8.

private property as possible rather than defending Newcastle's empty castle. That the Duke was despised by a large majority, not only within the working but also the middle and ruling classes, surely did not make their decision any harder.[440]

Newcastle assessed the situation differently and tried to charge the local Magistrates with dereliction of duty. They got back at him by ensuring that he did not get a seat on the Special Assize. After Newcastle then complained to the king, who chose to ignore him, they unsuccessfully tried to remove him as Lord Lieutenant of the county.[441]

The other noteworthy claim made by the unknown author of the letter to Newcastle, that the Mayor at least greatly contributed to the outbreak of serious rioting on Monday and Tuesday by calling the meeting in the Market Place,[442] was frequently stated, for example in the introduction speeches at the Special Assize:

> 'It appears that [...] a public meeting was held connected to the question of Parliamentary reform; but it does not appear that that meeting led to what afterwards followed. Though, when a multitude of persons assemble together for any particular purpose, it frequently happens, that misguided men will take the opportunity of committing acts totally foreign to the objects for which the meeting was convened, and resort to grievous outrages upon those who may differ with them in

---

440 See Beckett (a); pp. 124-7: Beckett's deliberations regarding this subject focus on the jurisdictional question, but he also concludes that 'town and county magistrates decided to sacrifice the castle to protect the town.'

441 Bryson p96; Gaunt (a); pp. xlii/90/93: The offended Duke wrote in his diaries 'Strange to say my name is not mentioned in the Commission – I have never yet seen a Commission in which the name of the L[or]d L[ieutenan]t of the County is not inserted amongst the first as a matter of course'. Regarding the attempt to remove him from office he wrote: 'The Fact is that they wanted to drive me out of the office & Knowing that I am not a cringer they Expected that I Should at once resign on receiving Such an insult – I would willingly do so, did I not fear the mischief that might be done by my Successor in the Office –'. See Welch (b); p. 2: Eventually Newcastle's 'reluctance to move with the times' did lose him the office of Lord Lieutenant in 1839.

442 NeC 5026: The letter strongly implied that the escalation was provoked deliberately by the mayor. The well-known and frequently quoted phrase 'England expects every man to do his duty' that had been printed on the bills advertising the meeting on Monday was allegedly used 'in the meaning of the great Admiral [Nelson] who first used it [at Trafalgar]', i.e. calling to 'Burn, Sink, and Destroy, all who oppose you.' See NeC 5016: Parsons had described usage of said 'memorable' phrase as animating and exciting'. See Nottingham Corporation; p. 99: Manson also claimed that the mayor had spurred on rioters, though as this allegedly happened after he had been attacked and injured, this seems rather unlikely.

> opinion, either with a view to revenge their private malice, or to gratify their evil desires for rapine and plunder.'[443]

It seems likely that events would have escalated on Monday whether or not a public meeting had been called. The local authorities may have actually hoped that by holding a mass meeting they might have a chance to control the crowds. This could be deemed naïve,[444] but the accusation that the middle class proponents of the Reform Bill deliberately provoked a riot is conclusively contradicted by their later conduct, especially their rather crucial role in quelling the riots.

In any case, such accusations played a substantial role in a hearing which began in August 1832 at the Special Assizes in Leicester. It had to decide the outcome of the compensation claim by the 'Duke of Newcastle v. the Inhabitants of the Hundred of Broxtowe'.[445] Newcastle's lawyers argued and legally proved that the Castle was situated in the Hundred of Broxtowe in the county of Nottinghamshire[446], making not the inhabitants of the town of Nottingham but those of the Hundred of Broxtowe liable to pay compensation.[447]

Newcastle's lawyers did their utmost to blame town officials for the riots, as at the public meeting 'advantage was taken of that assemblage, and of the excitement in the minds of the lower orders of people'. To call such a meeting, 'likely to have increased the disorder', was referred to as a mistaken remedy, such as a 'drunkard does, who when intoxicated, takes another glass of brandy to sober himself.'[448]

One of Newcastle's lawyers explained that:

> '[...] in my humble opinion nothing was more dangerous and absurd than to invite twenty thousand men together at such a period. They can't deliberate under such circumstances; they can only move upon their passions; and if they were all

443 *Journal*; 7th January 1831.

444 See ibid; 15th October 1831: The *Journal* was highly critical of the decision to hold a meeting and speculated that the town's officials relied too much on the ability of the speakers to 'control' the crowds and 'ease' their emotions and failing to realise that 'mischief was intended'.

445 Hicklin; pp. 1-5 (appendix): John Musters of Colwick Hall also claimed compensation. The case was tried at the Lent Assizes in 1832, but the outcome was not referred to in the examined records.

446 Ibid; p. 10 (appendix): As were Brewhouse Yard and Standard Hill.

447 Ibid; pp. 2/42 (appendix): According to an Act of Parliament in 'any place where a building shall be pulled down, damaged, or destroyed, the inhabitants of the hundred in which the destruction shall be committed, shall be liable to yield the full compensation to the owner thereof.'

448 Ibid; pp. 6/17-8 (appendix).

philosophers, instead of being men without education, and if they were all as wise as Sir Isaac Newton himself, they could no more form just opinions than so many children taken from their cradles.'[449]

In this logic the town's officials were responsible for the direct action as for the 'uncontrolled mob, who are always subject to the worst passions' rioting was described as the 'natural' reaction:

> '[...] for such is the nature of man, which no dictation will alter – it was natural, he would say, when vast numbers of men were thus assembled together, that they should be subject to an ebullition of violent passion, and be hurried on to do wrong and violence.'[450]

Following these attacks on the Duke's political enemies, his lawyers 'called [...] for full compensation, [...] which means the sum of money as will restore this Castle to its original strength, form and substance.' They demanded £30,000 as a 'lowest sum' as the castle had always been 'in good repair'.[451] On the second day of the hearing the jury reached the verdict to grant Newcastle £21,000,[452] a result that seriously displeased him.[453]

3.3. The Third Reform Bill

The debate about parliamentary reform did not end with the rejection of the Second Reform Bill. Reformists now demanded the appointment of further Peers to change the balance of power within the House of Lords:

> 'Something must be done, and that speedily too, or distrust will soon breed anarchy, confusion and bloodshed. A majority of forty-one ought not to be allowed to stand in the way of the people's claims. The only alternative a counterpoise by a fresh creation of Peers [...].'[454]

---

449 Ibid; p. 97 (appendix).

450 Ibid; p. 7 (appendix).

451 Ibid; pp. 15-6 (appendix). See Gaunt (a); pp. 172/174: In April 1824 Newcastle wrote that when he inspected the Castle he 'found it in very bad repair – the Joints open, the balustrades [...] fallen down, the flag pavements broken up & all in a very dilapidated state'. In August of the same year some maintenance work had begun.

452 Hicklin; p. 103 (appendix).

453 Gaunt (a); pp. 94-5: '10th August 1832: My cause for damages from the Hundred [...] was decided yesterday [...]. The verdict of the Jury, £21,000 damages – This [amounts to] nothing Equal to what I expected = The lowest I expected was 25 – or thought perhaps 30 000 might be obtained – not that 60,000 would rebuild & reinstate the Castle – The Cost to the County for the law expenses [sic] will be £2000 & they tell me not less to me – I am glad that the business is over.'

454 *Mercury*; 15th October 1831.

A new draft of the Reform Bill passed the Commons but Grey's government collapsed when the king did not intervene after the Lords threatened to reject it again. But as Wellington failed to install a Tory government, Grey forced the king to threaten the Lords with the appointment of new Whig Peers. Faced with this prospect, the passing of the so called 'Great Reform Act' was ensured by the abstention of the majority of the bill's opponents in the Lords.

In consequence fifty-six 'rotten boroughs' were disenfranchised, whilst further thirty constituencies lost one MP each. These seats were mainly redistributed to industrial areas including Birmingham, Manchester, Leeds, Sheffield, new London metropolitan districts and parts of Scotland.

Huge differences in constituency sizes remained. Three quarters of the borough constituencies had fewer than 1,000 voters, a further 35 fewer than 300, whereas Liverpool had 11,000. With the disappearance of some of the 'rotten boroughs', landed magnates like Newcastle did lose influence; however the Duke retained power in both Houses as he kept sponsoring candidates in constituencies like Newark. Altogether there were at least 70 constituencies still controlled by individual patrons. As voting was still done in public, it remained easy to monitor and sanction. Corruption flourished after 1832 just like it did before.

Hernon's claim that 'the Great Reform Act became law, but [...] did not alter very much' is further supported by looking at the size of the electorate in most parts of England. After the Reform Bill the franchise was held in counties by male 40s freeholders, male £10 long lease-holders and male £50 short leaseholders; in the boroughs all male £10 householders were eligible to vote, whilst those who held a borough before 1832 vote retained it, as long as they lived where they were part of the electorate. By these restrictions all women and 'the poor' were 'well and truly excluded' whilst only one in seven adult males had the right to vote.[455]

On the size of the electorate in Nottingham the reform had little impact. Thomis estimated that about 1,000-1,500 burgesses were disenfranchised, mostly those who were honorary but non-residential. They were replaced by about 1,200-1,500 new voters who fulfilled the criteria of being male £10 householders but had previously not been part of the electorate.[456]

455 Dinwiddy; pp. 46-9/68; Hernon; pp. 68-9; Welch (a); p. 1; Welch (b); p. 4/12.

456 Thomis (a); p. 235-6. Referring to methodological problems in calculating the size of the electorate he states that 'neither before nor after the Act could anyone state [...] the exact number of voters.' Before 1832 the number fluctuated as many were temporarily disfranchised whenever in receipt of parish aid. After 1832 the town continued to have a relatively 'broadly-based franchise, which was to help make possible the election of Feargus O'Connor in 1847.'

'Overall [the Whigs] gave a certain amount away, including a considerable number of Tory pocket boroughs; but there was no large-scale transfer of power from one class to another. The landed interest retained, and in some ways strengthened, its hold over the greater part of the electoral system, and the share of power allotted to middle-class interests was no more than a subordinate one.'[457]

Despite its very moderate content, there were bonfires and celebrations in Nottingham as the Reform Bill was passed. However, the mood quickly changed as it became clear that the 'Humbug Bill' was not going to have any impact on the plight of the majority of the population. Whatever hopes had been held and expressed, they apparently quickly disappeared. Among the policies of the reformed parliament was the Poor Law of 1834, by which eventually all forms of relief payments were abolished, leaving the poorest with no other option, aside from illegalised expropriations or starvation, than to enter a workhouse.[458]

'This policy was regarded by working people as a thoroughly heartless attack on the comfort, dignity and customary rights of the poor; and it was also interpreted by some as an attempt, by a parliament representing employers of labour, to induce workers to accept low wages as the only alternative to the workhouse. [...] A further aspect of what seemed to be a kind of offensive [against] the working classes [...] was the action taken against trade unions, [e.g.] the transportation of [...] the "Tolpuddle Martyrs"'.[459]

In June 1842 Newcastle had a conversation with an unemployed stockinger:

'He supposed that the object was to drive the people into a revolution, that both parties were alike & that between them the [...] intention was to crush the poor man = His last wages were 15s a week, out of which he had to pay 9s a week for frame rent, 2s for house rent & 8p ½ for needles leaving him the remainder to live upon – he said it was worse than nothing [...] because then he must go to the Bastille [the workhouse].'[460]

---

457 Dinwiddy; p. 55.

458 Bryson; p. 96; Dinwiddy; p. 71-2; Gray; p. 34; Pinchbeck; pp. 84-6.

459 Dinwiddy; p. 73. See Thompson; p. 908: The reformed House of Commons launched various policies aimed to break the trade unions. It was said that those who pampered the unions 'when they could be subservient to their purposes, were now endeavouring to crush the Trades Unions.'

460 Gaunt (a); p. 132.

The Reform Bill became anything but popular, not only among the working classes, but also among some of those who were supposed to gain political influence from it. Newcastle wrote on the 17th September 1832:

> '[...] a complete reaction has taken place at Nottingham – [...] the bulk of the tradesmen [...] now perceive that by the late Reform Bill they have lost Much & gained nothing – They are now greatly incensed against the authors of the deceit & [...] They Say now that nothing but revolution can Set them right'.[461]

[461] Ibid; p. 96.

4. Looking at and glimpsing into the crowds

4.1. Dreading the crowds

A 'misguided mob'[462], 'rascals'[463], an 'infuriated rabble'[464]. Using labels such as these to describe the Reform Rioters was common practice among many of their contemporaries. Modern accounts of the Reform Riots still show contempt for the 'hooligans',[465] the 'crowd of Goose Fair rowdies'[466].

An insight into the depiction of the rioters by their contemporaries can be gained by studying the rather crude work *The Crowd* by Gustave Le Bon, who attempted to develop a 'scientific' concept of crowd psychology. The French psychologist and sociologist, whose entire work is based on racism and sexism,[467] wrote at the turn of the nineteenth century.

In *The Crowd* Le Bon summarised many prevalent middle and ruling class anxieties of what became the industrial proletariat. It can therefore be seen as the culmination of a century of post-1789 discourse regarding the nature and the role of crowds in societies which were undergoing constant socioeconomic turmoil.

Le Bon was obsessed with the forthcoming end of civilisation, brought about by crowds.[468] He does not explicitly define his concept of civilisation, but only provides a detailed picture of its negation. However this indicates that Le Bon equates a civilised person with the figure of the self-sufficient bourgeois male, a patriarch exercising power over his family as well as himself, individual and independent in the sense of being the sole master of himself, i.e. the designer of his own fate, not only free from subordination in social relations but also in total control of his own emotions, instincts and lusts.[469] For Le Bon the crowd is the negation of this delusion, striving for nothing but a 'primitive communism' which inevitably will bring about the destruction of civilisation.[470]

---

462 *Journal*; 15th October 1831.
463 Gaunt (a); p. 84.
464 Hicklin; p. 125.
465 Thomis (a); p. 222.
466 Gray; pp. 34-5.
467 See e.g. Le Bon; pp. 75-6.
468 Ibid; pp. 6-10.
469 Truman; p. 22: This concept of bourgeois masculinity is contradicted by the capitalist mode of production as every individual has to sell commodities on the market (and be it only her/his own labour), i.e. every person is entangled in and has to adapt to a complex system of social relations.
470 Le Bon; pp. 8-10/206. On this idea he bases the concept of a 'cycle of the life of a people', an absurd philosophy of history: 'To pass in pursuit of an ideal from the barbarous to the civilised state, and then, when this ideal has lost its virtue, to decline and die, such is the cycle of the life of a people.'

He thought the late nineteenth century to be a 'critical moment' of 'transition and anarchy', a point in history when the 'Era of Crowds' had already begun and 'the power of the crowd is the only force that nothing menaces'. In this era the 'religious, political, and social beliefs in which all the elements of our civilisation are rooted' were allegedly already being destroyed one by one whilst 'entirely new conditions of existence and thought as the result of modern scientific and industrial discoveries' were being created.[471]

Such ideas had been mirrored in some statements commenting on the Reform Riots. Hicklin's description of an early stage of the riots in which he emphasises the wickedness of the rioters by contrasting their barbaric actions with the sacred ones of the churchgoers, is echoed in Le Bon's concept of the disintegration of society. Hicklin was also very fond of conjuring up apocalyptical themes, for example when he described the destruction of the castle as an 'infernal incantation', a 'tremendous sacrifice to the demon of anarchy and crime'.[472] Other commentators also see events during the Reform Bill Crisis as a real threat to the fabric of society, for example Newcastle, who fears that the nation might be 'overthrown';[473] the editors of the *Mercury,* who dread 'anarchy, confusion and bloodshed';[474] or Wellington, whose anxiety focuses on the annihilation of 'all property' which he believes will result in mass starvation.[475]

Even though there are traces of Le Bon's apocalyptic fantasies in the descriptions of and commentaries on the Reform Riots, they reflect much more his ideas about the nature of crowd psychology, which are based on the belief that:

> '[...] an agglomeration of men presents new characteristics very different from those of the individuals composing it. The sentiments and ideas of all the persons in the gathering take one and the same direction, and their conscious personality vanishes. A collective mind is formed [...] a single being, and is subjected to the Law of the Mental Unity of Crowds.'[476]

The crowd, this new being, is supposed to be driven by the 'unconscious qualities of character' of the individuals that constitute it, its intellect 'not an accumulation of the individuals' intellects but a replacement of the same by the 'collective unconsciousness'. Le Bon lengthily fantasises how these 'unconscious qualities of character' are based on the individuals' 'race'. He

471 Ibid; p. 6.
472 Hicklin; p. 160/165.
473 Gaunt (a); pp. 80-1.
474 *Mercury*; 15th October 1831.
475 Hernon; p. 61.
476 Le Bon; pp. 15-6.

equates the loss of self-control with childishness, the 'barbarism' of 'savages' and with femininity.[477] Central is the assumption that the unconscious nature of a crowd's characteristics determine the same to 'accumulate [...] stupidity', whilst the persons in the crowd 'yield' to their 'instincts' and develop 'a sentiment of invincible power'. In a crowd 'every sentiment and act is contagious', the crowd is 'the slave of impulses which it receives' as long as these 'are presented in a way [a crowd] can grasp with its non existent intellect'. The individual has become an 'automaton', no longer guided by will and reason, able to act autonomously, but rather guided 'by means of suggestion and contagion of feelings and ideas in an identical direction' and has a 'tendency to immediately transform the suggested ideas into acts'.[478]

Such ideas about crowds are referred to at length by contemporaries of the rioters. The judge in the Special Assize saw it in the 'nature of man, which no dictation will alter' that in crowds where 'vast numbers of men were [...] assembled together', people's behaviour changes and they become 'subject to an ebullition of violent passion'. It also seemed to be a fact that whilst in a crowd, individuals 'can't deliberate [...]; they can only move upon their passions'[479] and give 'vent to their passions.' It had also been suggested that in crowds the individuals' intellectual capabilities disappear: 'and if they were all philosophers, [...] they could no more form just opinions than so many children taken from their cradles.' The rioters were not seen to act autonomously but depicted as having been 'Set on',[480] by impulses given to them, for example by the message of an uprising in London and propaganda of reformists and radicals. Claims were also made of rumours spreading through the Nottingham crowds, seamlessly transforming themselves into actions. The initial outbreak of violence was described by the *Mercury* as a result of the 'multitude [becoming] very easily excited' by a 'report [which] caused some of [Hedderly's] upstairs windows to be broken'.

The rioters were also accused of savage behaviour by some of their contemporaries who stated that some persons in the crowds showed a 'spirit worthy of the barbarians of the darker ages'.[481] Such ideas were also prominently featured by Le Bon. According to him every 'cultivated individual' in a crowd: 'is a barbarian – that is, a creature acting by instinct

---

477 Ibid; pp. 18-21/55/158. See ibid; p. 31: 'Crowds are everywhere distinguished by feminine characteristics, but Latin crowds are the most feminine of all.'

478 Ibid; pp. 20-24/29/65-6/108-9/158: Le Bon's crowds are 'a new being in itself, an unreasonable, credulous creature, unable to tolerate discussion nor contradiction, open to suggestions [...]. The crowd can only think and act in extremes, be it adoration or hatred, sacrifice or slaughter.'

479 Hicklin; p. 7/97 (appendix).

480 Gaunt (a); p. 93; Hicklin; p. 97 (appendix); *Mercury*; 15th October 1831.

481 Hicklin; p. 164; *Mercury*; 15th October 1831.

[...], a grain of sand amid other grains of sand, which the wind stirs up at will.'[482]

The metaphor of the wind stirring up and guiding the sand was of high importance to Le Bon who wrote at length about the leaders of crowds, who can use various methods to guide crowds and use them according to their own agenda.[483] Such ideas were also referred to in 1831, be it in the *Mercury's* report of 'the lads' being 'mere instruments of more powerful agency' or in the obsession with identifying ringleaders, such as the tales of the mysterious stranger who is said to have stirred up the crowds in the Market Place,[484] or the depiction of George Beck as a de facto military commander of the crowd that burned down Lowe's mill.[485]

Le Bon's concept of crowd psychology was, as he understood it, the 'scientific' summary of anxieties which were also referred to in various accounts by the rioters' contemporaries, opponents and proponents of parliamentary reform alike. Both groups were apparently terrified by crowds, whose character and actions were constructed as the negation of civilisation.

4.2. Spotting faces in the crowd

The sources examined in this research process depict the rioting crowds as an amorphous mass rather than a congregation of individuals. Therefore the available evidence that can shed some light on these individuals' identities is fragmentary at best, though there is some information which allows a cautious debate as to who the rioters were, also contributing to educated guesses about their motivations (see 4.3.). However, the rioters themselves remain almost completely silent.

Furthermore, a second problem distorts any picture that emerges when analysing the available data: with one exception all the persons about whom some information is available are male, even though there is scattered, but conclusive evidence that women participated very actively in the Reform Riots.[486]

If they had not, this would have been an astonishing anomaly as women have always defied gender hierarchies by engaging in direct action like strikes and riots as well as having a crucial role in the organisation of the working classes.[487] Furthermore women were explicitly mentioned by the

---

482 Le Bon; p. 24.

483 Ibid; pp. 114-25: Especially these passages in Le Bon's work have been of much interest to various fascist and other authoritarian movements.

484 *Mercury*; 15th October 1831.

485 *Journal*; 7th; 14th; 21st January 1832.

486 *Mercury*; 15th October 1831.

487 O'Brien; pp. 8-11; Thompson; p. 70.

Secretary of State to have possibly been among those who destroyed the castle.[488]

In spite of this, historical as well as contemporary accounts do ignore women fighting in the Reform Riots, with a few remarks in the *Mercury* standing out as rare exceptions. Women are mentioned as having been present in the late afternoon and evening of Sunday 9th October when there was fighting in the town centre, as well as on Monday 10th, when 'females' participated in making a banner. The materials used to fashion the banner also make it highly likely that these women were, like those 'young men' with whom they collaborated, working in the textile industries. There is one piece of evidence directly referring to the active participation of women in the fighting: it is mentioned that one woman was seriously hurt when the Yeomanry charged into the crowd which had smashed the gates to Wollaton Park.[489]

The only woman named in connection to the Reform Riots is Elizabeth Hunt, a 30-year-old who was accused of having received some loot from the attack on Colwick Hall.[490] Due to this lack of evidence, any emerging picture of the rioters is gender biased and therefore of limited validity.

In order to be able to use the available data it will be assumed that those male persons about whom information is available, i.e. those who were prosecuted for their alleged involvement in the riots (even though it is likely that not all of them will have actually taken part in the direct action), are a representative sample of the men who did take part in the Reform Riots.

The *Mercury* drew 'great consolation' from their claim that 'the middle classes of society, those who were most likely to receive the franchise [...] remained peaceable and quiet'.[491] The rioting crowds were described by Manson as being drawn from 'the lower classes of this Town'.[492]

This does seem to be supported by the evidence examined, which formed the basis for drawing up a list of twenty-nine persons.[493] Of three of those people, neither age nor occupation are known. Of a further sixteen, there is no information regarding their occupation. Of the remaining ten persons, one is unemployed or 'seeking work', another 'works in a factory'. Two others are in work although it is unclear in what trade, one person is simply described as a 'labourer'. Among the remaining five are a framework knitter, a bobbin and carriage maker, a boatman, a brickmaker and one person who stated in his trial that on the day of his arrest he 'went to work

---

488 See Hicklin; p. 173: '[...] he, she, or they may be apprehended and convicted'.
489 *Mercury*; 15th October 1831.
490 DDFSI/134.
491 *Mercury*; 15th October 1831.
492 NeC 4998.
493 See 3.1. Of further eleven persons only their names and the fact that they were acquitted are known.

[...] to gather rags'. Referring to data recorded in later years, in this case the 1841 census records, it appears that at least three more of the twenty-nine also worked as framework knitters, whilst others apparently worked in manufacturing trades, other branches of the textile industry, such as lace making, or were employed as agricultural labourers. Given this information, it is possible that a few of those persons, for instance the framework knitters, may have held the status of free-men and therefore may have been eligible to vote, although they may also repeatedly have been disenfranchised, for instance whenever they were in receipt of parish aid. It seems likely that none of them would have been amongst those £10 householders who could have hoped to join the electorate as a consequence of the Reform Bill's success. It can therefore be assumed with ample surety that the vast majority of rioters would have been excluded from the right to vote before as well as after the 1832 reform.[494] In the case of Elizabeth Hunt her exclusion from the franchise would not only have been based on property and social status but also on gender.

Of the twenty-six persons whose age is known, twelve are 25 and younger, and a further twelve are 26-35 years old. Another person is 38, the oldest 50 years old. In a previous study, also using information regarding alleged rioters' ages and occupations, Wigley concluded that:

> '[...] the rioters [...] were neither misbehaved youths nor vagabonds, but drawn from an age group [defined by Wigley to be 17-27] capable of feeling and knowing its own interest, yet one peculiarly liable to displays of physical bravado, and more likely to hold strong views than detailed political opinions.'[495]

---

494 DDFSI/134; NeC 5052; *Journal*; 7th; 14th; 21st January 1832; Thomis (a); p. 235-6; Thomis/Preston/Wigley; p. 97. See also *1841 UK Census Collection*: When examining the census records, those ten persons whose occupations had been specified in the earlier sources, as well as another four who had been deported following their convictions, were not further investigated. Of the remaining fifteen it was possible to identify five persons with ample surety, all working in the textile industries. Regarding a further four persons it was not possible to identify them beyond reasonable doubt in the census records. However, it was possible in these cases to narrow down the search to three to five candidates. All but one fit the outlined profile, working e.g. as agricultural labourers, framework knitters, in manufacturing trades etc. The only one who does not quite fit into this picture is stated to be a watchman. A tenth man who could be identified in the census records, although also in this case some doubts remain, appears to be the most affluent person, by 1832 possibly even qualifying as a £10 householder. He is described as a shopkeeper, but it remains unknown whether he had also been a shopkeeper in 1831, and if he was it is notable that none of the sources refer to this fact. Given the remaining uncertainties, the data from the census records was not added to the Appendices.

495 Ibid: In Wigley's sample he knew the age of eighteen persons.

Wigley's first claim is relevant as the available data does indeed indicate that the claims of the rioters being a 'gang' consisting 'of all the low and bad characters [...] pickpockets [...] and the vile and worthless of every description, who had come to the town under the hope of picking up some plunder at the races'[496] is contradicted by the records. However, his interpretation of the fact that the majority of the persons were between 17 and 27 years old constructs a meaningless contrast between 'strong views' and 'detailed political opinions' and connects without any further debate gender and age with a certain concept of masculinity. The fact that also in the sample analysed in this text the majority of persons, eighteen of twenty-six persons, are younger than 28 years, can be interpreted much more prosaically as the consequence of the living and working conditions in a town in which the average life expectancy was twenty-two.[497]

The most detailed information about individuals in the crowds can be found on those who were hanged. George Beck was a 20-year-old from Wollaton, employed as a boatman. 'When a boy, he was tap-lad at the Eclipse public-house, Chapel-bar, and afterwards served the bricklayers as a labourer.'

George Hearson, aged 21, was born in Nottingham. His father died when George was still a child. George married 'about a year and a half' before his execution, but had no children.[498]

> 'He was put to business of a bobbin and carriage maker, he has subsequently worked at the manufacture of lace, and has always been connected with this staple fabric of our town.'[499]

George was allegedly known to have, despite his 'honesty', been 'led into intercourse with idle and disorderly persons, and in the prize ring of his vicinity, he obtained the appellation of "Curley Hearson."'

John Armstrong, aged 26, was allegedly present at Colwick Hall, the Castle and Beeston Mill. John was born in Pleasley, outside Mansfield. John's parents, three brothers and two sisters lived in Nottingham, on Millstone Lane. John was, like his father, a framework knitter. He was engaged to a woman from Nottingham, where he had lived the two years prior to his execution, although before he moved frequently, having lived in 'Mansfield, Derby, and other places, when employment could not be obtained in the town.' He was described as being of good character with 'civility, sobriety' and 'said honesty throughout life.' After receiving his verdict he was described to have been 'cheerful and resigned, expressing to his family a hope that he should meet them in a better world.' In a letter to

---

496 *Mercury*; 15th October 1831.
497 Thomis (a); p. 24.
498 DD763/8.
499 Ibid.

his father he provided a list of names he wished to be his bearers, thanked a Rose Martin for having confirmed his innocence and expressed his hopes to 'meet [his mother and brothers] at the right hand of God.'[500]

From the available data certain cautious conclusions can be drawn, keeping in mind that the evidence is rather fragmentary, especially regarding the participation of women in the riots. It appears that the rioters were part of the working classes, mostly working in low paid and rather precarious occupations. They lived in the town or its suburbs and nearby villages,[501] although it was not unusual that persons moved during their lives. Finally it seems to be likely that only few 'if any, of the Nottingham rioters, received the vote' in 1832,[502] least of all the rioting women.

4.3. Rioting for the Reform Bill, bounty or class war?

The question to what extent the rioters were interested in the Whigs' Reform Bill, or whether they instead took advantage of the situation as an excuse to set off on a few days of plundering, divided the rioters' contemporaries.[503] The *Journal's* interpretation is an example for the latter:

> 'The rejection of the Reform Bill by the House of Lords has stirred among the rabble a spirit of enterprise, and accordingly they have commenced the work of destruction [...] by burning and looting. Among the excesses which they committed, may be named, the firing of the Duke of Newcastle's Seat in Nottinghamshire, under the pretence of he, being an Anti-Reformer, must forsooth be marked out for destruction. [...] But to identify the [...] rioters with reform, is really to disgrace their name, and to injure the cause.'[504]

Many commentators, proponents as well as opponents of the Whig's Reform Bill, denied or played down the political dimension of the riots. For them the tale of rioting hooligans, 'the very dregs of society', engaged in 'a series of disorganised, riotous episodes [...] into which people were drawn by a mixture of motives, none of which concerned the reform of Parliament' was a useful version of events. Such an interpretation was adopted by some of the proponents of parliamentary reform who were afraid to have their cause weakened by the riots and this depiction was a welcome opportunity

500 Ibid; See *Journal*; 14th October 1832.
501 One of the shortcomings of this research is that no systematic attempt was made to identify the homes of the alleged rioters. See Beckett; p. 133: Based on his research, he assumed that the majority of rioters were living and working within the town's borders.
502 Welch (b); p. 12.
503 Thomis/Preston/Wigley; p. 84.
504 *Journal*; 15th October 1831.

to distance themselves from the 'depraved criminals'. On the other hand, the bill's opponents were also interested in this version of events as it helped to understate 'the extent of national revulsion' regarding the outcome of the vote in the Lords.[505]

A recurring element of these interpretations was blaming country people and strangers, 'the vile and worthless of every description, [who came] to the town [to pick] up some plunder'.[506] This was made easier as Goose Fair and the Nottingham Races were scheduled for the week of the riots. Both events attracted many country people and furnished 'opportunities for petty crime', especially as the 1831 Goose Fair is supposed to have been the largest up to that date.[507]

It is indeed likely that the coincidence of the Reform Bill being rejected during Goose Fair did fuel the riots, be it merely for the fact that the town was cramped with even more people than usual. Even though the empirical evidence indicates that the majority of those who took part in the riots lived and worked in the town, they will have been joined by others who came to Nottingham for Goose Fair and the Races.[508] It is therefore not denied that people living in out-of-town suburbs and villages took part in the direct action; however this cannot be used to explain the occurrence of the riots. In Derby there were no major festivities, yet there were massive riots, whilst in Birmingham a mass meeting was called during an annual fair but no riot broke out.[509]

Furthermore, the tale of the riots being primarily perpetrated by out-of-town 'thieves', wanting to gain bounty can be dismissed with ample surety, simply as it does not appear that a lot of bounty was taken. Although some pieces of jewellery were removed from Colwick Hall, as well as food, alcohol and, on a few occasions, money, during the numerous attacks on private houses and shops, Lowe's mill or indeed the castle, no significant expropriations took place. A desire for plunder can also not account for the rioters' choice of targets, especially not for the attack on an almost empty castle or the House of Correction. It is the choice of these targets which exemplify that politics, to be understood in a broader sense than just parliamentary politics, lay at the very core of the riots.

According to Beckett 'the rioters had quite specific targets'. He understands the rioters 'objectives' within 'Nottingham' as being 'limited to

---

505 Thomis (a); pp. 226-7; Thomis/Preston/Wigley; p. 84.

506 *Mercury*; 15th October 1831.

507 Thomis (a); pp. 227-9; Thomis/Preston/Wigley; p. 84.

508 *Journal*; 7th; 14th January 1832; *Mercury*; 15th October 1831: There had been various reports of persons e.g. sleeping in the fields, indicating they lived outside of town. Furthermore witnesses giving evidence at the Special Assize stated that they came to Nottingham on Tuesday 11th October to see the ruins of the castle.

509 Thomis/Preston/Wigley; pp. 84-5.

harassing anti-reformers'. Therefore Beckett cannot explain rioters' motives for targeting Whig-supporting John Webster's house and also the attack on Colwick Hall remains 'obscure' to him, stating that being 'a local tory was enough'.[510] Preston also argues that it were 'almost exclusively anti-reformers who suffered', whilst Wigley states that aside from targeting known opponents of the Bill 'the crowd's activities were designed to wreak revenge upon the chargers of high prices, givers of low wages and upholders of law and order.'[511]

An attempt to classify the rioters' choice of targets utilising Preston's and Wigley's categories[512] indicates that the crowds struck their targets very accurately indeed.[513] Furthermore this strongly suggests that the crowds were motivated by more than just the rejection of the Whigs' Reform Bill, thereby indicating (further) motives for attacks which remain obscure if the riots are just understood as a hunt for Tories and other anti-reformers.

Four premises can be placed within the category: 'upholders of law and order'. There was the House of Correction, the houses of constables Berry and Webster and finally Colwick Hall,[514] property of the hated Magistrate Musters. That the latter was also a known 'arch Tory'[515] and that Berry had signed the anti-reform petition exemplifies that most targets chosen by the crowds fit more than just one category. For Beckett, the attack on Webster's house seems to have been the result of 'indiscriminate or mistaken violence' as he had not signed the anti-reform petition and had voted for Whig candidates.[516] Seen in context with the attack on Musters the Magistrate

---

510 Beckett; pp. 122/136-7.

511 Thomis/Preston/Wigley; pp. 85-6/98-9. See *Mercury*; 15th October 1831; Nottingham Corporation; pp. 114/186-7; *Journal*; 14th January 1832: It is noteworthy that the crowds were almost exclusively not 'wreaking revenge' on people but targeted property instead. They confined themselves to destroying windows, smashing all sorts of means of production, wrecking furniture and setting fire to buildings. Exceptions were those constables, the Yeomanry and from Tuesday morning the Hussars who tried to suppress the rioters. Furthermore Manson's servant, the mayor, Enfield's clerk, a Mr. Barber and Musters' son were injured. There is the account of people in the crowd attacking Lowe's mill wanting to 'frizzle' its owner, but even aside from the circumstances in which these testimonies were given, it is unknown whether Lowe would really have been attacked by the crowds if he had been found at his mill.

512 See Appendix III.

513 Thomis (a); p. 227: Thomis is highly sceptical whether the crowds were targeting Reform Bill opponents accurately. According to him, the rioters attacking Lowe's Mill were so unfamiliar with the layout of the town that they almost attacked an Alfred Lowe of Highfield House.

514 See Appendix I; *Mercury*; 15th October 1831.

515 Bryson; p. 95.

516 Beckett; p. 122.

and the House of Correction it is however very possible that the attack was not an error but that Webster was targeted as he was an 'upholder of law and order'.

The vast majority of the targeted buildings were owned by persons who had political affinities with the Tories, for example they had voted for Tory candidates, like Loveitt and North had previously done,[517] and/or they were known opponents to parliamentary reform. Some premises would have been widely known as being the property of reactionaries like Lord Middleton or the Duke of Newcastle. What political opinions were expressed in the *Journal* would also have been public knowledge, sufficiently explaining why their office windows were smashed. The names of the owners of nine targeted premises, among them the druggist Hedderly and Sharp the mill owner,[518] had been published by the *Review* as signatories of the anti-reform petition. The properties of the ten other persons whose names were published in the *Review* were apparently not targeted by rioters. Of those, two lived in Carlton and one in Cropwell, places where there were no riotous crowds. As two others were farmers it is likely that they also lived in areas where rioters had not been active. A further four persons are only mentioned by name, making it futile to guess why their properties were not attacked. It seems odd that a Mr Marriott was not targeted although he lived in St. James Street. However the house of the hosier Mr Swann was attacked, who lived on the same road. This could indicate that Swann's house was mistaken for belonging to Marriot, which could explain both these apparent errors. Similarly the property of a Mr Wood, about whom no other information could be found in the sources examined, formerly belonged to the hosier Kewney who had voted for Tory candidates, which might explain why Wood's house lost some window panes.

To determine with ample surety why the premises of the baker Smith and the grocer Prickard were visited will require further research. However, it can be speculated that they could have been 'chargers of high prices'[519] and/or possibly Tory-supporters, although it is also possible that the crowds simply needed to expropriate provisions.[520] The Greyhound and a number of other pubs were probably visited simply because they were

---

517 See ibid; p.124 for a list of a number of targeted persons who had 'plumped tory'.

518 See Appendix XI.; *Review*; 30th September 1831. See also Staveley/Wood: Their map depicts eleven mills in the Forest area. A number of them were within easy reach of any crowd operating in the area, indicating that Sharp's was targeted deliberately.

519 See Rudé; p. 88: Since 1830 wheat prices had been very high.

520 See *Damn your charity ...*; chapters 3.2./3.4.: for further information on the well-established practice of food expropriations and the equally common practice of punishing those perceived to cause and/or profit from high food prices.

situated along the route of a hungry and thirsty crowd. That crowds also called on the Whig Needham was probably a genuine mistake as it is mentioned that the rioters thought his house to be the home of Wright, a known Tory.[521]

This evidence strengthens the claim that the rioters targeted very specific premises rather than just being on a plundering rampage. It has yet to be sufficiently established whether some targets were picked because their owners were 'chargers of high prices [and/or] givers of low wages'. It is for example possible that Lowe's mill was targeted not just because of its owner's support for the Tories but also as he might have been a 'giver of low wages' or caused socioeconomic distress to workers in other ways.[522] However, even if it is assumed that all targeted premises were either owned by 'anti-reformers' (like the castle or Manson's house) or visited to expropriate provisions (like the *Greyhound* pub), this cannot explain the attack on the House of Correction or constable Webster. These attacks alone verify that some targets were chosen as they fell into a second of Wigley's categories, as the constable as well as the House of Correction were, symbolically and practically, upholding law and order. Therefore it is not only possible to conclude that the rioters were primarily motivated by political issues, but that these included a hatred of law enforcement as well as a loathing of Reform Bill opponents.

A number of things indicate that it was indeed hatred of the Reform Bill's opponents rather than disappointed enthusiasm for the Whig's Reform Bill that lay behind the attacks on Tory supporters and Reform Bill opponents. According to the Reform Bill all women and all the urban as well as the rural poor would continue to be excluded from the franchise. As the evidence discussed in 4.2. indicates that the overwhelming majority or even all rioters belonged to at least one of these three categories, the question remains why any of them should have fought after a bill had failed which aimed to enfranchise their 'masters'.[523]

A certain degree of support for the Reform Bill among the working classes is undeniable, as demonstrated for example by the number of signatures for pro-reform petitions. Thomis argues that working people in Nottingham

---

521 *Mercury*; 15th October 1831.

522 In any case it is noteworthy that one of the few places in Nottinghamshire where textile commodities were produced in a factory setting was targeted and destroyed. See *Journal*; 14th January 1832: Although the claims at the Special Assize of people wanting to 'frizzle' Lowe have to be treated with the utmost care, they might indicate that Lowe was especially despised.

523 Thomis (a); p. 222; Thomis/Preston/Wigley; p. 86. See Dinwiddy; p. 63: In fact working class radicals were not delighted about their masters' prospect of the franchise but argued that the Whigs were extending the suffrage to the middle classes 'in order to prevent the lower classes from obtaining their rights'.

were simply fooled by Whig propaganda that managed to mobilise them in support of a Reform Bill they did not 'fully understand' even though there had been 'detailed accounts in the local press'.[524]

That the places which saw the 'worst' rioting, i.e. Bristol, Nottingham and Derby, all had 'powerful Whig elements',[525] indicates a level of truth in Thomis' claim regarding the effectiveness of Whig propaganda. However, it may very well be that working class people had been mobilised *against* the opponents of the Reform Bill rather than *for* its contents:

> '[...] Whigs and moderate reformers were paradoxically assisted, during the Reform Bill crisis as a whole, by the fact that the Tory aristocracy put up such stubborn resistance. This helped to divert popular attention from the limitations of the Bill and to focus it on the evils of oligarchy and boroughmongering and 'Old Corruption.' The riots at Nottingham and Bristol [...] can be seen as reflections of this orientation'.[526]

It is difficult to ascertain to what degree the loathing of the opponents of the Reform Bill was the result of successful Whig propaganda or of strategic considerations by members of the working classes. The latter can be supported by numerous accounts of 'the poor men of this town' hearing 'the newspapers read every night in thousands, during the progress of the Reform Bill'.[527] There had also been fierce debates within the working classes whether to support the Reform Bill as a 'stepping stone' or whether to oppose it in order to campaign for more radical political and social reforms.[528] In any case, these accounts indicate that among the people of Nottingham, far from being a mass of ignorant plebs as implied by Thomis, political discussions were a well-established part of everyday life.

To many of these people, excluded from the franchise on account of their gender, social status and/or wealth, irrespective of the Reform Bill's fate, the reorganisation of constituencies may have been the most relevant aspect of the Whigs' Reform Bill. Although this was not an attack on the

---

524 Thomis (a); p. 230. See Field; p. 399: The *Date Book*'s description of the rioters merges such a tale of ignorant plebs with the one of the vile strangers: 'Goose fair had attracted [...] an unusually large number of strangers, amongst whom were a considerable body of evil disposed persons. These [...] needed but a colourable pretence to induce the ignorant and unreflecting of the Reformers to join them in the commission of acts of devastation and plunder; and unfortunately, the obstinacy of the House of Lords too soon gave them the alluring incentive.'

525 Thomis/Preston/Wigley; p. 86.

526 Dinwiddy; p. 67.

527 Nottingham Corporation; p. 117.

528 Dinwiddy; p. 63: Hunt said at Bolton in April 1831 'it certainly was all very good, very liberal, but would it get the people something more to eat?'

principle that landed magnates controlled a considerable number of MPs, many in the working classes will probably have welcomed the prospect of reactionary extremists like Newcastle losing some influence in the wake of a successful Reform Bill. According to this interpretation, many rioters knew exactly that they were to gain little or nothing from the Reform Bill, but they also knew that at least some of the hated boroughmongers were to lose from it. To these people, the defeat of the Reform Bill in the Lords would have marked yet another occasion when the boroughmongers successfully defended their power and privileges, which evidently led to feelings of frustration.

The emerging picture of the Reform Rioters in Nottingham indicates that they were part of the working classes, lived most of the time in a situation of extreme economic plight and were fighting not for the Whig's parliamentary reform but against what they identified as the 'old corruption'. They targeted boroughmongers and their middle class allies whilst also venting their anger on institutions and executors of law and order and possibly on those who were perceived to underpay members of the working classes and merchants who were perceived to charge unusually high rates for their commodities. Therefore the Reform Riots:

> '[...] fit as well into the 18th century tradition of popular protest as into the 19th century of political demonstration, but their scale and virulence, and the possibilities of escalation [...] gave more than an ordinary shock to contemporary opinion. The aftermath of the riots was thus a working class suspicious of its erstwhile leaders, a middle class chastened and fearful for the future, an aristocracy not only disillusioned with the Whigs but frightened and truculent, and a government determined above all things to maintain order.'[529]

For Thompson the Reform Bill Crisis marked a crucial point in the development of a class consciousness amongst the working classes, i.e. the realisation of an identity of interests amid working class people and the realisation that these interests are in conflict with those of other classes. It is this second criterion which was greatly advanced during the Reform Bill Crisis, particularly as the proponents of reform, though trying to stimulate mass agitation for reform, 'carried in their knapsacks a special constable's baton', determined to stop revolution by any means necessary. For Thompson it was the mixture of repression during the Reform Bill Crisis and disappointment after the Reform Bill had been passed, that served as a catalyst for the acknowledgment of class antagonism.[530]

529 Ibid; pp. 101-2.
530 Thompson; pp. 887-91/913.

In this interpretation the Reform Riots mark a transitionary moment in the history of the British working classes, in which class antagonism[531] was becoming more widely acknowledged, as more people overcame the illusion that their masters' interests were 'identical to [their] own'. This interpretation was also shared by some of those whose property had been targeted during the riots, as they saw the direct action as an indicator for a 'growing political consciousness of the lower classes'. Thomis refers to *Review* articles stating that a war of 'labour against property' could develop.[532]

> 'One reason why [...] working-class resentments were consolidated to a greater extent into a broad sense of hostility towards the propertied and employing classes was the political settlement of 1832. Previously [...] there had been [...] the idea that the middle and working classes constituted together an excluded "people" [...]. After 1832, the line which separated the political nation from those outside it corresponded closely to the social dividing line between the propertied classes and the rest of the community.'[533]

Whether there really was the threat of a revolutionary uprising during the Reform Bill Crisis,[534] has been questioned.[535] Some symbols of power and oppression, like prisons, were attacked in Nottingham, Derby and Bristol. On the other hand, there were reports that some rioters continued to idolise institutions like the monarchy. There are recurring accounts that rioters thought they were backed by the king and doing his will, exemplified by the reports of people singing the national anthem in the Market Place on Sunday evening.[536] Whether or not such accounts were accurate and representative, it appears undeniable that even if there was some level of 'revolutionary excitement' in Britain during the Reform Bill Crisis, it was not enough to ignite a genuine revolutionary insurrection.[537]

---

531 Engels (a); p. 8921 (see MEW volume 22; pp. 291).
532 Thomis (a); pp. 227-9; Thomis/Preston/Wigley; p. 84/86.
533 Dinwiddy; p. 78.
534 Rudé; pp. 87-8.
535 Wright; pp. 46-7.
536 Thomis/Preston/Wigley; p. 85. See *Mercury*; 15th October 1831. Singing 'God Save the King' as the Hussars first showed up on the scene could have been the result of a multitude of reasons, including a tactical decision to try to deescalate the situation by pledging loyalty to the crown. See 'The Ten Propositions'; p. 164: It is however likely that the very persistent myth of a wise king, misled by those around him, which had frequently been referred to e.g. in the earlier stages of the English Revolution, was actually believed by a number of people.
537 Wright; p. 47: 'If there had been genuine revolutionary excitement in the country, needing only a spark to set it alight, then surely the ignition would have been provided by the Bristol riots.'

This is even more tragic as the chances for a successful large scale insurrection may have been comparatively good due to the weakness of the 'forces of law and order':

> '[...] even a weak and disorganised revolutionary impulse has some chance of success of the forces of the established order are impotent. Such an opportunity was available in 1830-2, since public order in the provinces was in the hands of local officials, who lacked professional police forces and were obliged to rely on semi trained yeomanry and untrained special constables. [There] was an overall shortage of troops, who therefore had to be moved quickly from one trouble spot to another. Simultaneous risings in widespread areas of the country would probably have proved too much for the inadequate machinery of public order. The fact that the machinery was never really tested reveals the weakness of the revolutionary threat. [...] As it was, order was soon restored.'[538]

[538] Ibid; p. 46-7.

Conclusions

Both core theses could be confirmed. The analysis and debate of the examined evidence indicates that the people who fought in the Reform Riots were members of the worse-off sections of the working classes, mostly working in low paid occupations, some of which (like framework knitting) long having suffered from almost constant depression. The failure of the Whigs' Reform Bill in 1831, i.e. its rejection by the Lords, although triggering the Reform Riots, cannot fully explain the events. The bill had little to offer to male rioters and even less to the fighting women. It appears that many rioters' actions were not primarily driven by disappointed enthusiasm for the moderate reformists' cause, but rather hatred of those perceived as reactionaries, be it boroughmongers like Newcastle or their middle class allies like Manson. Furthermore, the people expressed their hatred of institutions and executors of law and order by engaging in direct action against them, demonstrating that resisting repression also motivated many rioters.[539]

However, even though it is indicated by the choice of some targets[540] and scattered pieces of evidence like the alleged defiant outcry when the final crowd was dispersed on Tuesday night,[541] the used evidence does not allow us to conclusively link the undeniable socioeconomic distress of the working classes in Nottingham with the events during the Reform Riots.

It is furthermore unclear whether those who fought during those three days of October 1831 had an agenda other than the punishment of the aforesaid groups, be it desiring a specific kind of parliamentary reform or more progressive social and political changes, maybe even a revolutionary reorganisation of social relations. But regardless what intentions and convictions some rioters may have had, the Reform Riots were not a revolutionary uprising.

Nevertheless, the rioters did cause considerable damage to property, which was estimated to have amounted to about £50,000 to £60,000 in Nottingham alone.[542] Tragically there were a number of deaths: the two children found dead in the ruins of the castle the day after its destruction, and the three persons murdered on the gallows in February 1832. A further six were deported and a number of persons, including Thomas Auckland severely injured. Compared to the massacres which ended the fighting in

539 See also Appendix XIV.: for a number of other examples demonstrating that the people of Nottingham repeatedly challenged the upholders of law and order.

540 Whether or not some targets, such as a grocer's store or Lowe's mill, may have been chosen to take revenge on 'chargers of high prices' and/or 'givers of low wages', remains unknown.

541 See *Mercury*; 15th October 1831: '[We] may as well die where we are as to go home and be starved.'

542 *Journal*; 15th October 1831.

Bristol, rioters in Nottingham suffered less for their decision to engage in collective acts of direct action, but this does not make the deaths, injuries and transportations any less tragic.

One crucial result of this research project seems to be that the people in the crowds did act autonomously, defying the calls for calm and moderation by members of the middle and ruling classes.[543] They acted conscious of the fact that striking 'at the security of property' did not 'lay open to attack the cottage of the mechanic as well as the mansion of the rich', that burning the property of aristocrats like Newcastle, capitalists like Lowe and middle class merchants like Hedderly did not 'render any place the object of destruction.'[544] Indeed, the claims that the Reform Riots had a catalysing effect on the acknowledgment of class antagonism seem to be supported by the available evidence. The majority of the rioters' targets had been middling, respectable opponents of the Reform Bill. But not only them, but also the middling, respectable proponents of the Reform Bill were the recruiting ground for special constables and Yeomanry, determined to swiftly repress any challenge of the social order. The Whigs' Reform Bill did succeed in adjusting and stabilising the class compromise of 1688 by incorporating more respectable people, but in doing so it encouraged autonomous action and organisation within the working classes.[545]

Prominent among the many shortcomings of this text is a lack of theoretical deliberations. A multitude of terms and concepts have been used implicitly and explicitly without being defined and debated in sufficient detail, like the unfolding of industrial capitalism, class consciousness, crowd psychology, or concepts of masculinity (to name but a few).

That problem aside, the two most significant shortcomings of this research project are: firstly, the lack of evidence that records the views of members of the working classes, forcing the deliberations regarding the rioters' motives to be grounded in circumstantial evidence only. Further records need to be accessed in an attempt to identify documents which may rectify this problem. Secondly, the evidence regarding women's living and working conditions as well as their active involvement in social struggles was insufficient to form the basis of anything other than a superficial debate. Further research in this area will be crucial.

---

543 See *Mercury*; 15th October 1831. See 2.2.: those official speakers addressing the crowds during the meeting on Market Place do not appear to have been part of the urban poor.

544 *Journal*; 21st January 1832. See idem; 15th October 1831: Those rioters who smashed the windows of the *Journal's* office were also well aware that the paper did not 'promote the best interests and welfare of all classes of the community.'

545 Thompson; pp. 230-1: '[...] the disappointment and frustration that followed 1832 were this time to lead to a specifically working class political movement, Chartism.'

It is always fruitful and enjoyable to dig into the turbulent history of Nottingham and to rediscover pieces of its long history of social struggles. At a time when revolution is even less likely than during the Reform Bill Crisis this is particularly important.

Researching and celebrating our common history of dissent, radicalism, revolutionary sentiment and rioting defies attempts to construct an image of Nottingham based around brainless slogans like 'Proud, Ambitious, Safe'. This is even more reason not only to engage in these activities but to rediscover them as part of our heritage and thereby reclaim the latter from those who do not consider machine breakers to be role models, but fictional archers fighting for good governance.

To constantly question, rewrite and deconstruct our understanding of past formations of social relations can help us to think and act beyond the present one. Therefore, historic research is not only enjoyable, but knowledge of past struggles can help us fighting present ones.

In the end, I cannot help but feel some regret that Nottingham Castle has been rebuilt. Despite ever more excellent projects being hosted and undertaken there,[546] the castle's charred ruins would have remained an inspiring embodiment of Nottingham's tumultuous history, as well as allowing continued usage of this most marvellous description of the city:

'Old Nottingham,
the Land of Lud,
Of Lace and Stockings,
of good ale and wassail,
Bold hearts,
and *once* a venerable Castle.'[547]

---

546 Indeed, in recent years much time, resources and space have been allocated to exciting projects. It can only be hoped that the days are over when the galleries were dominated by permanent reminders of Torvill and Dean and temporary exhibitions of Russell Crowe's pants.

547 Hicklin; titlepage.

Appendices

I. Timeline of the Nottingham Reform Riots

This list has been compiled using information from the *Mercury* and the *Journal* (both dated 15th October 1831), Colonel Thackwell's account of the riots (printed in Wylly's *The military memoirs of ... Joseph Thackwell...*), Field's *Date Book* and the account of the riots given in Fellows and Freeman's *Historical Records of the South Nottinghamshire ... Yeomanry* .... For detailed references see chapters 2.1.-2.4.

Entries marked * refer to estimated time(s), etc.

Entries marked ** refer to persons/properties owned by persons who had signed the anti-reform petition and whose names had been published in the *Review*, September 30th 1831.

Street/area	**Venue**	**Occupation of owner/ occupant**	**Event(s)**	**Day(s)**	**Time**
?	?	N/A	news of the Reform Bill's rejection reach Nottingham	Sat 8th Oct	8.30pm
High Street	Post Office/ near the *White Lion*	N/A	mail coach arrives	Sun 9th Oct	10am
Clumber Street	Hedderly's shop**	druggist	some kind of fracas occurs (possibly windows are smashed)	Sun	morning
Pelham Street	?	N/A	brick thrown at Manson**, hitting his servant	Sun	morning
Clumber Street and its side streets	N/A	N/A	crowds grow; disputed whether stones were thrown at windows before about 7pm	Sun	late afternoon
Clumber Street; Market Place and side streets	N/A	N/A	spectators turn up; police unable to control crowd; possibly stones thrown	Sun	dusk (6 to 6.30pm*)
Bridlesmith Gate	Ward's shop**	druggist	windows smashed	Sun	7pm
Clumber Street	Hedderly's shop**	druggist	windows smashed; riot act read; Mayor's head struck by stone	Sun	7pm
Stoney Street	Manson's house**	M.D.	windows smashed	Sun	7-7.30pm

Street/area	Venue	Occupation of owner/ occupant	Event(s)	Day(s)	Time
Market Place; Long Row	Wright's shop**	book-seller; printer	windows smashed; shop demolished; mayor's leg hurt	Sun	8.30pm
Market Place	N/A	N/A	Oldknow and Wilkins try to calm crowd	Sun	after arrival of the military
Market Place; various parts of the town	N/A	N/A	military repeatedly disperse crowds	Sun	evening; night
Leen Side	Brad-shaw's house**	whar-finger	targeted by rioters	Sun; Mon 10th Oct	in the course of the night
Mansfield Road	Sharp's house**	miller	targeted by rioters; food expropriated	Sun; Mon	in the course of the night
Charlotte Street	North's house	cheese-monger	targeted by rioters; food expropriated	Sun; Mon	in the course of the night
Chapel Bar	Cooke's house	grocer	targeted by rioters	Sun; Mon	in the course of the night
Pilcher Gate	Lowe's house	silk mill owner	targeted by rioters	Sun; Mon	in the course of the night
Long Row	office of the *Journal*	N/A	front windows partly smashed	Sun; Mon	in the course of the night
Pilcher Gate	Kewney's house	hosier	targeted by rioters	Sun; Mon*	in the course of the night*
Market Place	N/A	N/A	12-15,000 attend an official meeting; various reformist speakers address the crowd	Mon	late morning; midday*
Barracks	N/A	N/A	military standing by to suppress rioting	Mon	during the meeting on Market Place
The Park	?	N/A	another meeting is held; addressed by (a) person(s) unknown*	Mon	during the meeting on Market Place*

Street/area	Venue	Occupation of owner/ occupant	Event(s)	Day(s)	Time
on or near Market Place*	?	N/A	meeting in the Park ended; brief scuffle ends as group coming from the Park seizes banner from persons coming from Market Place	Mon	during the meeting on Market Place*
between Market Place and Hockley	N/A	N/A	a Hussar retakes the seized banner by riding into crowd	Mon	after the meeting on Market Place
Market Place	N/A	N/A	meeting is ended	Mon	1-2pm
?	N/A	N/A	town clerk advises military to stand down	Mon	2.30pm
Hockley	Smith's house	baker	windows smashed	Mon	between 2.30 and 3pm*
Hockley	Prickard's house	grocer	windows smashed	Mon	between 2.30 and 3pm*
Chesterfield Street	Berry's house**	constable	windows smashed; doors forced in; furniture damaged	Mon	between 2.30 and 3pm*
Derby Road	Webster's house	constable	windows smashed	Mon	between 2.30 and 3pm*
York Street	Loveitt's house	shop-keeper	windows smashed	Mon	between 2.30 and 3pm*
Mansfield Road	Clifton's house**	officer on half-pay	windows smashed	Mon	between 2.30 and 3pm*
The Forest	Sharp's mill**	N/A	flour and corn scattered; sails cut	Mon	between 2.30 and 3pm*
?	N/A	N/A	Mayor and Magistrates request military support	Mon	3-4pm
?	?	?	properties attacked; crowds are repeatedly dispersed	Mon	after the attack on Sharp's mill
Sneinton	?	N/A	people arm themselves with makeshift pikes	Mon	after the attack on Sharp's mill

Street/area	Venue	Occupation of owner/ occupant	Event(s)	Day(s)	Time
Colwick Hall	N/A	Magis-trate	mansion attacked, numerous rooms trashed	Mon	6-7pm*
St John's Street	House of Correc-tion	N/A	attack repelled	Mon	7.30pm
Wheeler Gate	Woods' house; formerly in posses-sion of Kewney	?	windows smashed	Mon	7.30pm
Nottingham Castle	N/A	N/A	stormed	Mon	7.30pm
Nottingham Castle	N/A	N/A	set on fire	Mon	7.30-8pm*
Nottingham Castle	N/A	N/A	full ablaze; huge crowds gather to watch	Mon	9pm
Nottingham Castle	N/A	N/A	flames subside	Mon	midnight
?	?	N/A	Yeomanry mustered; special constables sworn in	Mon; Tue 11th Oct	in the course of the night
St. James' Street	Swann's house	hosier	windows smashed	Mon; Tue	in the course of the night*
Nottingham Castle	N/A	N/A	two children, Ellerby and Kilbourn, die in the ruins	Tue*	morning*
Nottingham Castle	N/A	N/A	soldiers engage a crowd; people fight back	Tue	morning
Derby Road	?	N/A	soldiers engage and disperse crowd	Tue	morning
Market Place and other locations	?	N/A	soldiers and yeomanry repeatedly engage and disperse crowds	Tue	early afternoon
near Derby Road*	Wright's house	banker	food and money expropriated	Tue	early afternoon
near Derby Road*	Charlton's house	Colonel	food and money expropriated	Tue	early afternoon
near Derby Road*	Storner's house	?	food and money expropriated	Tue	early afternoon
near Derby Road*	Need-ham's house	?	food and money expropriated; mistaken as Wright's house	Tue	early afternoon

Street/area	Venue	Occupation of owner/ occupant	Event(s)	Day(s)	Time
near Derby Road*	the *Grey-hound* and other pubs	N/A	food and alcohol expropriated	Tue	early afternoon
Beeston	Lowe's silk mill	-	trashed and burned	Tue	early afternoon*
near crossing of Beeston Road and Derby Road	gates to Wollaton Park	N/A	attack on Wollaton Hall repelled by cavalry charge; one woman severely injured; 15-17 prisoners taken	Tue	afternoon*
near the *Sir John Borlase Warren*	Chimley's Close	N/A	stones hurled at Yeomanry; they fire pistols; rioters withdraw	Tue	afternoon*
?	?	N/A	stones hurled at soldiers; one person arrested	Tue	afternoon*
Market Place; Bridlesmith Gate	?	N/A	Auckland shot in the chest by soldier	Tue	afternoon*
Market Place; Bridlesmith Gate	?	N/A	Hopkinson injured by the same bullet that struck Auckland	Tue	afternoon*
?	?	N/A	Mayor proclaims curfew	Tue	5pm
Market Place	N/A	N/A	no crowds on the streets	Tue	7pm
near the river	?	N/A	a last crowd dispersed	Tue	midnight

II. Alleged rioters

This table compiles information about alleged rioters, many of whom were tried at the Special Assize in January 1832. The data was excerpted from three issues of the *Journal*, dated 7th, 14th and 21st January 1832, the document NeC 5052: *Schedule of Prisoners...*, and primarily the document DDFSI/134: ... *Calendar of the Prisoners....* Furthermore a few details were taken from Thomis/Preston/Wigley; p. 97 and Beckett (a); p. 132. Although these sources also entail information about other prisoners, the following tables only list information about those who were indicted for offences related to the events which took place in the Nottingham Reform Riots, i.e. between the 9th and the 11th October 1831. Some of the persons listed in the tables had been out on bail.

Aside the persons listed below, the names of a further eleven persons were listed in the *Journal*, dated 14th January 1832:

> 'Grand Jury ignored the bill against James Bartle, W[illia]m. Scottoms, James Lowther, Samuel Horsley, W[illia]m. Butler Elliott, David Potts, John Allen, W. Armitage, Felix Testot, Thomas Allen, and Joseph Hind, who had all been out on bail, for the riot at Wollaton.'

Entries marked * contain information that is implied by the evidence without being explicitly stated.

Name	Age	Charge(s)	Occupation	Sentence
John Arm-strong	26	Riotously and tumultuously assembling [...] at Beeston, feloniously breaking and entering a certain silk mill, the property of William Lowe, and setting fire to the same.	framework knitter	hanged
George Beck	20	See above.	boatman	hanged
Charles Berkins	20	Riotously and tumultuously assembling [...] at Colwick, and unlawfully partly demolishing and destroying the dwelling house of John Musters, Esq. and feloniously breaking and entering the same, and stealing therein a quantity of jewellery and other articles, and feloniously damaging and setting fire to the household furniture in said dwelling-house [...].	?	transported*
Samuel Binks	17	See above.	?	discharged without trial*
Richard Branston	?	Riot at Wollaton (exact wording of the charge unknown).	?	not guilty

Name	Age	Charge(s)	Occupation	Sentence
Aaron Booth	19	Riotously and tumultuously assembling [...] in the parishes of Lenton, Beeston and Wollaton, to the disturbance of the public peace, and to the terror of the people.	?	discharged without trial*
Thomas Carlin the elder	50	Riotously and tumultuously assembling [...] within the extra-parochial limits of the Castle of Nottingham, unlawfully and maliciously setting fire to Nottingham Castle [...].	?	discharged without trial*°
Thomas Carlin the younger	28	See above.	?	discharged without trial*
Robert Cutts	27	See above.	?	not guilty
George Forman	?	Riot at Wollaton (wording of charge unknown).	?	not guilty
John Forman	23	Riotously and tumultuously assembling [...] at Beeston, feloniously breaking and entering a certain silk mill, the property of William Lowe, and setting fire to the same.	?	not guilty
William Freeman	22	Riotously and tumultuously assembling [...] at Colwick, feloniously breaking and entering the dwelling house of John Musters, Esq. and stealing therein one gold comb, the property of the said John Musters.	?	not guilty
William Green	30	Riotously and tumultuously assembling [...] in the parishes of Lenton, Beeston and Wollaton, to the disturbance of the public peace, and to the terror of the people.	?	discharged without trial*
Thomas Grundy	42	Lowe's mill (exact wording of the charge unknown).	?	not guilty
Thomas Harrison	17	Riotously and tumultuously assembling [...] Colwick, and [...] partly demolishing and destroying the dwelling house of John Musters, Esq. and [...] breaking and entering the same, and stealing therein a quantity of jewellery and other articles, and feloniously damaging and setting fire to the household furniture in said dwelling-house [...].	?	not guilty
George Hearson	22	Riotously and tumultuously assembling [...] at Beeston, feloniously breaking and entering a certain silk mill, the property of William Lowe, and setting fire to the same. & Riotously and tumultuously assembling [...] at Colwick, [...] breaking and entering the dwelling house of John Musters, Esq. and stealing therein a quantity of jewellery and other goods [...] and [...] setting fire to [it]..	bobbin and carriage maker	hanged

Name	Age	Charge(s)	Occupation	Sentence
William Hitch-cock	33	Riotously and tumultuously assembling [...] at Beeston, feloniously breaking and entering a certain silk mill, the property of William Lowe, and setting fire to the same.	?	not guilty
Elizabeth Hunt	30	Receiving this comb [see William Freeman], knowing it had been stolen.	?	discharged without trial*
Henry King	17	Riotously and tumultuously assembling [...] at Beeston, feloniously breaking and entering a certain silk mill, the property of William Lowe, and setting fire to the same. & Riotously and tumultuously assembling [...] at Colwick, feloniously breaking and entering the dwelling house of John Musters, Esq. and stealing therein a quantity of jewellery and other goods [...] John Musters and [...] setting fire to [the same].	?	not guilty
William Kitchen	26	Riotously and tumultuously assembling with others at Beeston, feloniously breaking and entering a certain silk mill, the property of William Lowe, and setting fire to the same.	'seeking work'	transported*
Henry Linley	19	See above.	works 'in a factory'	not guilty
Valentine Marshall	17	Riotously and tumultuously assembling with others at Colwick, [...] breaking and entering the dwelling house of John Musters, Esq. and stealing therein a quantity of jewellery and other goods, the property of the said John Musters and wilfully and feloniously setting fire to the said dwelling-house.	?	transported*
Joseph Shaw	35	See above. & Riotously and tumultuously assembling with others within the extra-parochial limits of the Castle of Nottingham, unlawfully and maliciously setting fire to Nottingham Castle, the property of the Duke of Newcastle.	?	not guilty
Thomas Shelton	38	Riotously and tumultuously assembling with others at Beeston, feloniously breaking and entering a certain silk mill, the property of William Lowe, and setting fire to the same. & Riotously and tumultuously assembling with others at Colwick, and unlawfully partly demolishing and destroying the dwelling house of John Musters, Esq. and feloniously breaking and entering the same, and stealing therein a quantity of jewellery and other articles, and feloniously damaging and setting fire to the household furniture in said dwelling-house then being, whereby a great part thereof was consumed and destroyed.	?	transported*

Name	Age	Charge(s)	Occupation	Sentence
Thomas Smith	34	Riotously and tumultuously assembling with others at Colwick, feloniously breaking and entering the dwelling house of John Musters, Esq. and stealing therein a quantity of jewellery and other goods, the property of the said John Musters and wilfully and feloniously setting fire to the said dwelling-house.	?	not guilty
Samuel Spencer	32	See above.	?	not guilty
David Thurman	26	Riotously and tumultuously assembling with others at Beeston, feloniously breaking and entering a certain silk mill, the property of William Lowe, and setting fire to the same.	on the day he 'went to work [...] to gather rags'	transported*
Adam Wagstaff	26	See above.	brick-maker	not guilty
Thomas Whitaker	24	Riotously and tumultuously assembling with others at Colwick, feloniously breaking and entering the dwelling house of John Musters, Esq. and stealing therein a quantity of jewellery and other goods, the property of the said John Musters and wilfully and feloniously setting fire to the said dwelling-house.	?	transported*

III. The rioters' targets

This table lists premises which were attacked in Nottingham and the town's neighbourhood between 9th and 11th October 1831. It furthermore suggests why the owners of these properties might have been targeted (see also 4.3.). Regarding the category 'Signed anti-reform petition' see also Appendix XI. The wide category 'Tory/Tory supporter' indicates for example that the person had voted for Tory candidates. The category 'upholders of law and order' is used for the Magistrate Musters, constables Berry and Webster or the House of Correction. This table has been compiled using information from a number of sources, notably various issues of the *Mercury* and the *Journal* and the articles of Thomis/Preston/Wigley and Beckett. It is probably not a complete list of the rioters' targets nor can it claim to provide more than incomplete suggestions as to why these targets were chosen.

Venue/ Owner	**Occupation of owner/ occupant**	**Signed anti-reform petition**	**Tory/Tory supporter**	**'Upholder of law and order'**	**Notes**
Berry's house	constable	✓		✓	
Bradshaw's house	wharfinger	✓			
Charlton's house	colonel				described as 'anti-reformer' (unspecified) by Thomis/Preston/Wigley
Clifton's house	officer on half-pay	✓			
Colwick Hall/John Musters	Magistrate		✓	✓	
Cooke's house	grocer		✓		
the *Greyhound* and other pubs	N/A				situated along the route of a hungry and thirsty crowd
Hedderly's shop	druggist	✓	✓		
Hicklin's house	publisher	✓	✓		
House of Correction	N/A			✓	
Kewney's house	hosier		✓		
Loveitt's house	shopkeeper		✓		
Lowe's house/Lowe's silk mill	silk mill owner		✓		
Manson's house	M.D.	✓	✓		

Venue/ Owner	Occupation of owner/ occupant	Signed anti-reform petition	Tory/Tory supporter	'Upholder of law and order'	Notes
Needham's house	?				he supported the Reform Bill, but his house was mistaken for John Wright's
North's house	cheesemonger		✓		
Nottingham Castle/Henry Fiennes Pelham Clinton, Fourth Duke of Newcastle	N/A		✓		
office of the *Nottingham Journal*	N/A		✓		
Prickard's house	grocer				unclear why he was targeted
Sharp's house/ Sharp's corn mill	miller	✓	✓		
Smith's house	baker				unclear why he was targeted
Storner's house	?				described as 'anti-reformer' (unspecified) by Thomis/Preston/Wigley
Swann's house	hosier				Swann voted for Whig candidates but his house was possibly mistaken for Marriott's, a signatory of the anti-reform petition who lived on the same street
Ward's shop	druggist	✓	✓		
Webster's house	constable			✓	voted for Whig candidates
Wollaton Hall/ Lord Middleton	N/A		✓		
Woods' house	?				unclear why he was targeted, but the house formerly belonged to Kewney
(C.N.) Wright's shop	bookseller; printer	✓	✓		
(John) Wright's house	banker				described as 'anti-reformer' (unspecified) by Thomis/Preston/Wigley

IV. The early nineteenth century electoral system

Wright briefly outlines some of the characteristics and oddities of the British electoral system before 1832:[548]

Elections only had to be held every seven years. In the balance of power between the government of the day, Commons, Lords and monarchy, the latter two institutions played a more active role than in later variants of the British version of the bourgeois-capitalist regime.

The House of Lords was a centre for various groups exerting power:

> 'Most ministers sat in the Lords; so also did the great landed proprietors, whose property included control of many constituencies. [...] Leaders of the army, navy, civil service, Church and local government also sat in the Lords.'

The role of the central government was extremely limited by modern standards:

> 'Administrations contended themselves with maintaining law and order, raising taxes, conducting foreign policy and defending the realm.'

Parliamentary constituencies were divided into boroughs and counties. Each county and most boroughs sent two MPs to Parliament. Each county-MP had to possess an assured annual income (for example land inhabited by tenants) of £600 (£300 for borough-MPs). In the eighteenth century there were 558 seats in the House of Commons (489 constituencies in England, 24 in Wales, 45 in Scotland). 122 MPs were sent by county, 432 by borough constituencies.

The electorate in counties consisted of those males who possessed the so called 40s freehold. In practice this could mean various things: mostly land ownership, but also holding office in church or state. County elections were primarily dominated by the landed gentry and aristocracy:

> 'Great landed families usually monopolised the county seats. Often two of the leading families would agree to share the representation and avoid the ruinous costs of a contested election.'

The electorate mainly consisted of better off tenants, shopkeepers or tradesmen, who were rarely willing to oppose the wishes of the landed magnates. If there was more than one candidate up for election, not only the threat of post-election sanctions, but also various forms of bribery (for instance offering free booze or coals), were used to ensure the preferred outcome of an election. Although political pressure or 'bloody brawls'

[548] Wright; pp. 1-12.

('electioneering could be a lively business') usually did the trick to guarantee the victory of the local magnates' favourite, post-election sanctions were used against rebellious voters ('open voting made rebels easily identifiable'). Such measures included the eviction of tenants, withdrawal of custom from tradesmen and shopkeepers, or the withholding of fees owed to solicitors, doctors and land agents.

The boroughs greatly varied in size and voting qualifications, being only uniform in their categorical exclusion of women. Only 22 of the 203 English boroughs had more than 1,000 voters; in a further 22, the electorate consisted of 500-1,000 persons. Eleven boroughs had 500 voters and the other 148 were known as 'rotten' or 'pocket' boroughs:

> '[...] that is, they were influenced or controlled by a patron or by the government. Some boroughs were tiny. All twenty-one in Cornwall, and most of those in Surrey and Sussex, had under 200 electors. Gatton had only six.'

Voting qualifications in the boroughs were complicated. There were five main classes of boroughs:

In 'Potwalloper boroughs' the vote was held by all men who had their own house and fireplace.

In 'Scot and lot boroughs' the vote was held by all male householders who paid local rates and were not on poor relief.

In 'Freeman boroughs' the vote was held by all males who had a freeman qualification produced for example by inheritance, marriage, apprenticeship, or purchase.

In 'Corporation boroughs' the vote was restricted to an oligarchy of corporation members.

In 'Burgage boroughs' the franchise was attached to piece of land and whoever owned that piece of land could vote:

> 'The most notorious of these was Old Sarum, a mound in Wiltshire with no houses. On election day, the seven voters met in a tent specially erected for the purpose.'

As electoral registers did not have to be kept before the 1832 Reform Act, the size of the electorate before that date is difficult to estimate. Nevertheless, Wright provides various figures. According to these, in 1800 about three per cent of adult males held the franchise, after the reform of 1832 only about one in 24 persons.

V. The Castle

Referring to a description in the Gentleman's Magazine, Hicklin described the interior of Nottingham Castle prior to its destruction:

> 'It is now many years since a Duke of Newcastle made any lengthened stay within the walls of Nottingham Castle. At the time it was noticed in the Beauties of England and Wales, about twenty years ago, it was inhabited by two ladies, in separate tenements. The rooms were of noble dimensions, and furnished in a half modern style. In the drawing-room, which commanded an extensive prospect, were heavy velvet curtains, and cabinets of the time of Louis XIV. The dining-room and the suite adjoining were, perhaps, the most ancient in the house. They were adjourned in the panels, the heavy carved work of which served them as frames. The staircase was a fine specimen of English oak and stone-work; but most of the pictures which had at one time adorned it were removed. One or two ancient helmets remained, as well as the long rolls of the genealogy of its noble possessor; but amidst these relics of the past there was no attempt to introduce modern art or comfort. An air of desertion pervaded the entire building. For many years past the Castle had been let by the noble owner as private residences. The last persons who occupied this spacious mansion, were Mr. Rawson and Mrs. Greaves, the latter of whom left in 1829; from which time until its destruction by the rioters, in October, 1831 it remained tenantless.'[549]

549 Hicklin; pp. 158-9. See Bryson; pp. 94-5 for information on the castle's lodgers. See Deering; pp. 170-99: His *History of Nottingham*, published in 1751, provides a detailed description of the Nottingham Castle.

VI. The attack on Colwick Hall

At the Special Assizes John Musters son, William gave a lengthy statement regarding events at Colwick Hall, which resulted in damages of £2-3,000:

> 'I was home on the 10th of October, when the mob arrived. I saw them approach up the park. I met them 150 yards from the house. [...] I said to them I hoped they would go away quietly. The mob behind struck at and pelted me, and I was obliged to retire. I received a blow to my right arm. I went into the house; my mother, and sister, and Miss de Fay were there. The mob commenced by taking up stones, and breaking the windows; they then forced the shutters in different parts of the house. They had spikes, or the tops of iron railing, which they brought with them; and they broke down our iron railing, to make use of to get into the house. They got into the house. [...] The mob destroyed everything they possibly could in the rooms they went into; they were the lower rooms principally. They entered the dining room, the little room my brother and I sat in, my mother's and father's bed room, and destroyed all the furniture. I informed my mother, sister, and Miss de Fay of the approach of the mob, and they went into the ball room. When I went again to find them, they were gone into the shrubbery, and were under the laurels. My mother's health was very delicate. The mob set fire to the house in the different rooms. The smoke was very great. The floors in my mother's room were very much burnt; that is an up-stairs room. My father's room was also burnt; they put the bed and furniture in this room upon the fire in the grate. They set fire to one of the corners of the room, where there was some gunpowder, which exploded. That fire burnt the furniture. The explosion produced an effect upon the walls, but did not burn any part. [...] The same was done in the drawing room; they had placed the chairs, and pillows off the sofa, and put them upon the fire in the grate. They burnt our coats and other things in the little room, but no part of the room was burnt. The floor of my mother's dressing room, my father's bed room, the drawing room, and the sitting room were not burnt. My mother's jewels were taken out of her dressing room. I lost a gold chain. A gold comb of my mother's was taken away. The mob came about five o'clock in the afternoon, and left about six. I saw them go away, shouting "Hurra".'[550]

---

550 *Journal*; 14th January 1832.

VII. Impressions of a burning castle

'About nine o'clock, the spectacle was awfully grand, and viewed from whatever point, the conflagration presented an exhibition such as seldom witnessed. The grand outline of the building remained entire whilst immense volumes of flames poured forth at the windows , and in some places were seen through the green foliage of the trees. Thousands of people thronged the Castle-yard and every spot that commanded a sight of the fire. [...] On the terrace round the upper basement, persons were seen like restless spirits, passing to and from and every now and again as the dense smoke caught the flames, a wild shout resounded in the air. The lower basement of the building to the westward is occupied by the servants' offices, kitchen, &c. and here a large fire was kindled. And lads enjoyed themselves in breaking windows and bringing forth everything of combustible nature, which was immediately committed to the flames. Doors, shutters, bottle racks, dressers were soon destroyed; and the work of devastation went on rapidly, whilst firebrands were carried into every part that could be reached. [...] The rain fell heavily, and the sparks came down in amazing quantities, so as literally to fall in showers. A stable or outbuilding next to the wall going into the Park, was also consumed.'[551]

'Between the hours of nine and ten, the conflagration had reached its height; the town was comparatively free from tumult, and thousands thronged the Castle-yard, to gaze with mingled feeling on the dreadfully novel spectacle. Volumes of flame issued forth from all the windows of the building; the dun-coloured smoke rose mist-like in rolling masses, among the pelting rain; showers of sparks were falling in all direction; the roofs were dissolving in streams of molten lead; on the terraces and walls men might be descried by the light of the fire, hurrying to and fro, like restless spirits, at some infernal incantation, while the blazing castle glared on the atmosphere from its rocky steep, amidst the darkness of the night, as a tremendous sacrifice to the demon of anarchy and crime. About midnight the fire began to subside, and the following morning witnessed this once noble edifice a roofless shell, every part but the walls having been entirely consumed [...].'[552]

---

551 *Mercury*; 15th October 1831.

552 Hicklin; p. 165.

VIII. The attack on Lowe's mill

At the trial of George Beck various witnesses stated their version of the events at Lowe's mill in Beeston:

> '[...] a large mob of several thousand persons went on the Derby Road, supposed with the intention of visiting Lord Middleton; but as they proceeded, it appeared that they were aware his Lordship was prepared to receive them. This caused a halt, and a cry was soon raised, 'To Beeston mill!' The prisoner would be proved on this occasion to have been carrying a tri-coloured flag, armed sometimes with a rail, at others with an iron bar. When the mob got to Beeston, the prisoner headed them, and on getting to the mill, he said 'Halt, front, this is the place; fall round and do your duty.' The mob immediately began to destroy and set fire to the mill. They broke the windows and destroyed everything in the mill. The mill and two houses were burnt, and the damage done was about £15,000.'[553]

> '[William Turton – an employee at Beeston mill] saw a mob of between two and three thousand persons, part of them three deep of forty men in the front rank, then two deep and afterwards a complete mob. George Beck was carrying a flag, and when they came to the mill, he said, 'This is the place,' and the mob threw stones at the windows.'

553 *Journal*; 14th January 1832.

IX. The shooting of Thomas Auckland

These accounts describe two versions how Thomas Auckland and Joshua Hopkinson were shot by one of Thackwell's Hussars:

> 'It was the performance of this duty (the escorting the prisoners through the town) that a man of the name of Auckland, a tailor and a pensioner, received a wound in the breast, having been shot, while offering some insult to an officer, or making an assault upon some of the party. (We have heard various versions of the story, one account being that the unfortunate man was drunk, and merely making some rude observations; another that the man actually made an assault; and a third that he was attempting a rescue: we know not which of these statements is correct, or whether there be any truth at all in any of them, but certain is, that the wounded man lay at the Infirmary yesterday in so dangerous a state, as not to be expected to recover.)[554]

> 'Whilst crossing the Market-place, the throng pressed upon [the Hussars], and turning into the Poultry, much abusive language was used, and stones were thrown. The officer who brought up the rear was much insulted and struck by a stone. Finding the mob press upon him he deliberately returned his sword to his scabbard, drew his pistol from the holster, and fired in the direction of High-street. The ball struck an old man, named Thomas Auckland in the chest, passed out at the shoulder, and then grazed the forehead of Joshua Hopkinson, of Arnold. Auckland had served many years in the 33d foot, and was severely wounded at the battle of Waterloo. He has resided for some time on Mansfield-road, in the enjoyment of a pension for his services, and carrying on the business of a tailor. He was conveyed to the Infirmary, where he still lies with hopes of recovery.'[555]

---

554 Idem; 15th October 1831.
555 *Mercury*; 15th October 1831.

X. The Special Assize

This incomplete summary of the procedures at the Special Assize has been compiled using three issues of the Journal, dated 7th, 14th and 21st January 1832, Tallents' description of events published in Gaunt's Politics, Law and Society... and the document DDFSI/134; the ... Calendar of the Prisoners.... As the indicted faced capital punishment for the kind of offences they were charged with, a verdict of guilty meant death by hanging, unless a 'recommendation to the Majesty's mercy' resulted in transportation to one of the colonies. Entries marked with * refer to persons who were 'recommended to his Majesty's mercy' after the end of the proceedings of the Special Assize.

Date	**Proceedings**	**Defendant(s)**	**Age(s)**	**Profession(s)**	**Verdict(s)**	**'recommended to his Majesty's mercy'**
Wed 4th Jan	official opening under heavy military protection	N/A	N/A	N/A	N/A	N/A
Thu 5th Jan	opening speeches	N/A	N/A	N/A	N/A	N/A
Fri 6th Jan	trials re: Lowe's Mill	George Beck	20	Boatman	guilty	no
Sat 7th Jan	trials re: Lowe's Mill	George Hearson	22	bobbin and carriage maker	guilty	no
		John Armstrong	26	framework knitter	guilty	no
		Thomas Shelton	38	?	guilty	no*
Mon 9th Jan	trials re: Lowe's Mill	Henry Linley	19	works 'in a factory'	not guilty	-
		John Forman	23	?	not guilty	-
		David Thurman	26	on day of arrest 'went to work [...] to gather rags'	guilty	yes
		William Kitchen	26	'seeking work'	guilty	yes

Date	Proceedings	Defendant(s)	Age(s)	Profession(s)	Verdict(s)	'recommended to his Majesty's mercy'
Tue 10th Jan	trials re: Lowe's Mill	Adam Wagstaff	25	Brickmaker	not guilty	-
		Henry King	17	?	not guilty	-
		William Hitchcock	33	?	not guilty	-
		Thomas Grundy	42	?	not guilty	-
		Thomas Smith	34	?	not guilty	-
Wed 11th Jan	trials re: Colwick Hall	Charles Berkins	20	?	guilty	no*
		Valentine Marshall	17	?	guilty	yes
		Thomas Whitaker	24	?	guilty	yes
Thu 12th Jan	trials re: Colwick Hall	Samuel Spencer	32	?	not guilty	-
		Joseph Shaw	35	?	not guilty	-
		Thomas Harrison	23	?	not guilty	-
		William Freeman	22	?	not guilty	-
		Henry King	17	?	not guilty	-
		Thomas Smith	34	?	not guilty	-
Fri 13th Jan	trials re: Nottingham Castle	Robert Cutts	27	?	not guilty	-
		Joseph Shaw	35	?	not guilty	-
	trials re: Wollaton riots	Henry Linley	19	works 'in a factory'	not guilty	-
		George Forman	?	?	not guilty	-
		Richard Branston	?	?	not guilty	-

XI. Miscellaneous

Estimated development of the population in Nottingham[556]

Year	1750	1801	1811	1821	1831	1841
Population (nearest 100)	ca. 10,000	28,800	34,000	42,400	50,700	53,100

List of signatories of the anti-reform petition

This list of those who had signed a petition 'against some of the clauses of the Bill [...] couched in terms of respectful moderation' was published by the *Review* eight days before the riots began:

Alexander Manson M.D.	John Parr, farmer, Cropwell
Job Bradshaw	Thomas Berry, constable
Thomas Marriott, St James-St.	N. Need, draper
C.N. Wright, printer	Butler, farmer
H.P. Ward, druggist	Hardstaff, farmer
John Hedderly, druggist	Hanbury, druggist
John Hickling	Sharp, miller
Capt. Clifton	Newham, farmer, Carlton
Brough, printer	Benj. Palmer
Samuel Bridger, Carlton	

> '[...] a friend [...] has furnished us with the following list [...]: the gentlemen who have viewed the reform bill "with the utmost anxiety and alarm," will unquestionably thank us for making known their names to the world.'[557]

A proclamation issued by the Duke of Newcastle

> 'The Lord Lieutenant loses not an instant in acquainting all [...] that he has this day retuned to Nottinghamshire. He is determined to repress with the strong arm of the Law, the perpetration of such base and nefarious outrages as have recently and for ever disgraced the Town and Neighbourhood of Nottingham; and he calls upon the Authorities and others immediately to communicate with him at Clumber, and of the Magistrates in particular he requires that they should give him the speediest and most regular accounts of everything that passes [...]. Clumber, Thursday Evening, Oct. 13, 1831.'[558]

---

556 Welch (b); p. 7. See Beckett (b); pp. 192-3 for more detailed figures.
557 *Review*; 30th September; 1831.
558 *Mercury*; 15th October 1831.

XII. Maps

Maps A and B demonstrate the consequences of the population increase for the building density.

Map A: Nottingham town centre c.1740 (Deering)

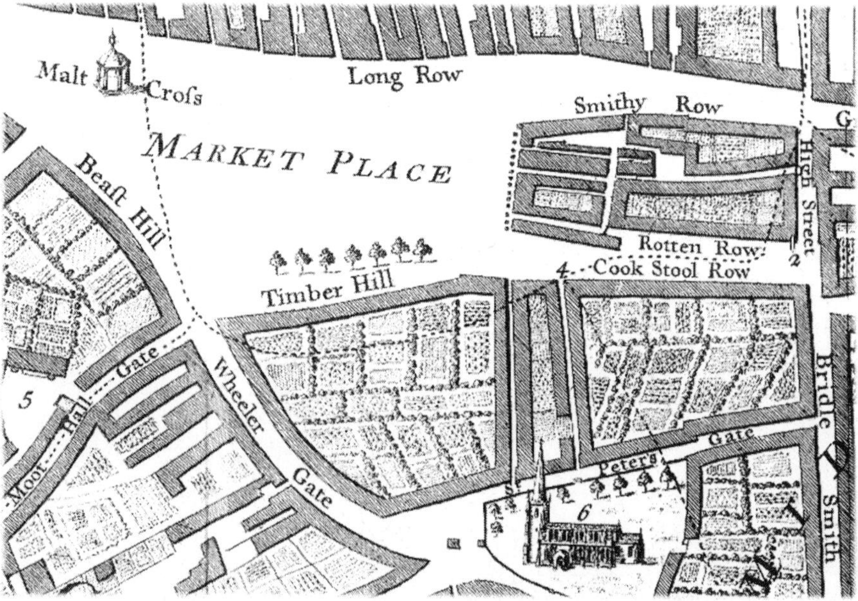

Map B: Nottingham town centre c.1830 (Staveley/Wood)

Map C: Overview of the Town of Nottingham (Staveley/Wood)

Map D: Town Centre and surrounding streets (Staveley/Wood)

Map E: The castle and surrounding streets (Staveley/Wood)

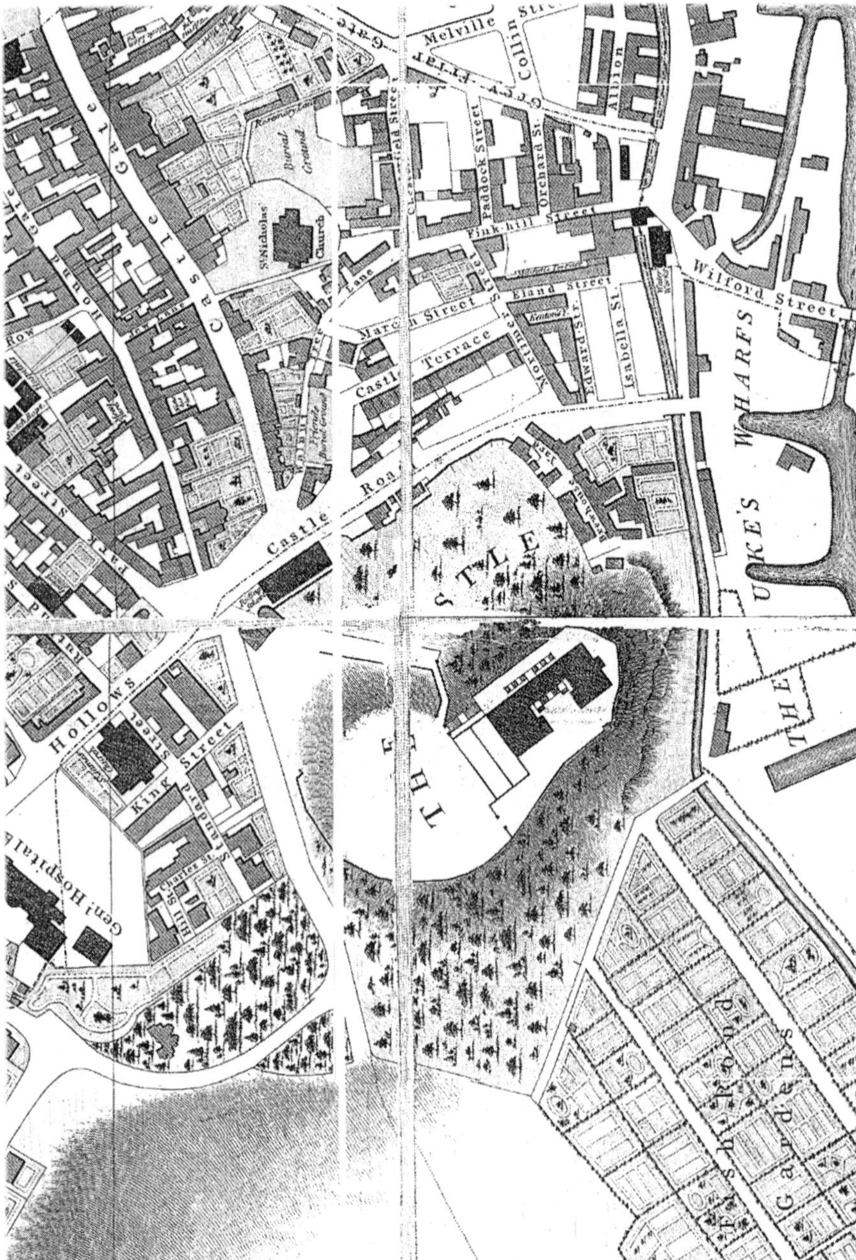

XIII. Images

Unless stated otherwise, these images were found in the database *Picture the Past* (www.picturethepast.org.uk).

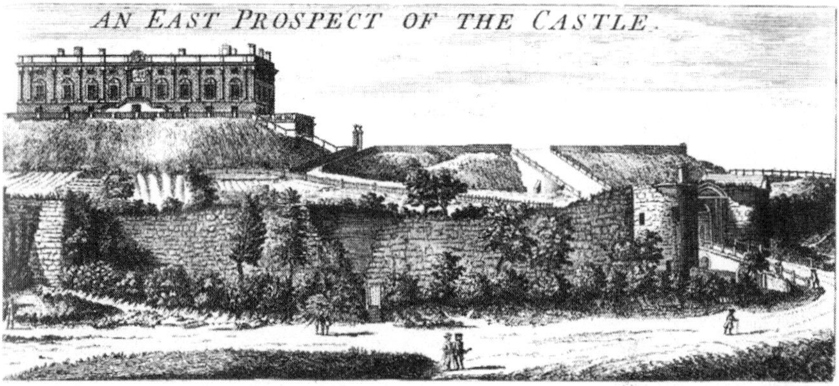

'An East Prospect of the Castle'; undated; in: Deering.

Nottingham Castle Lodge (gatehouse); c.1800.

Market Square/Market Place; c.1830.

House of Correction; c.1900. Unfortunately we could not find an image of the building as it would have looked when it was attacked in 1831.

Nottingham Castle on fire; 10th October 1831; top left: viewed from a field to the south-west; top right: viewed from the south; bottom left: viewed from the west by the river Leen; bottom right: viewed from the south.

Valentine Marshall's name scratched on the wall of the men's exercise yard; Galleries of Justice; photographed August 2010.

XIV. Timeline of riots in Nottingham 1766-1831

For details see Field's *Date Book of remarkable and memorable events....*

October 1766	High cheese prices result in severe **Food Riots**. One person is shot dead by the military. The events become known as the 'Great Cheese Riot'.
1767	The introduction of the 'spinning jenny', enabling a single worker to spin a multitude of threads, causes riots as workers fear for their livelihoods. The prototype and a number of **machines are destroyed**.
June 1779	The rejection of a bill to regulate the framework knitters' trade triggers serious riots. Over five days, **workers** from town and county **damage hosiers' houses and break frames**. The promise of negotiations ends the riots, but the hosiers' subsequent refusal to compromise leads to further direct action, only quelled after a large scale mobilisation of troops and special constables.
June 1780	During celebrations staged for the king's birthday, **armed military officers and locals clash** on Market Square, leaving a number of people severely injured.
June 1783	A drop in the rates of pay causes a riot by framework knitters. Over two days, **hosiers' windows are smashed** etc. Military repeatedly attack the rioters and although the crowds resist fiercely, they are finally subdued by the soldiers' swords and bullets. At least one person is killed, others severely wounded.
October 1787	A number of framework knitters **break a hosier's frame**.
May 1788	High prices trigger a **Food Riot.** 'Great quantities' of meat are taken.
June 1790	Quarrels over an **election** cause **rioting**. Soldiers fire into crowds, killing one man and wounding a number of other persons.
October 1790	Having their income yet again reduced by hosiers, framework knitters **attack several houses**. Troops arrest numerous rioters.
Autumn 1791	A number of framework knitters from the county assemble and try to negotiate with a hosier. Though unprovoked, **soldiers charge into the crowd of workers who fight back**, reinforced by numerous town dwellers. A brutal engagement leaves a number of people injured.
May 1792	High prices for meat trigger a **Food Riot**. Temporarily dispersed by military, rioters later reassemble, trash the Shambles and use the debris to create a huge bonfire in Market Square.
June 1793	A number of persons suspected of being supporters of the French Revolution are attacked in a field near the town. The same **royalists attack** the Mayor's home. One is shot dead, others injured.
July 1794	Over the course of a few weeks, **royalists attack** suspected radicals and democrats, e.g. laying siege to a cotton mill where republicans sought refuge. Royalists round up their opponents and 'duck' them under pumps on Market Square and in the Leen, torturing and almost drowning many persons. At least one dies following this ordeal.
April 1795	A **Food Riot** caused by high prices of meat is quelled by Yeomanry and Dragoons.
July 1795	Another **Food Riot** occurs, this time due to the high price of wheat. Rioters go round bakers' shops, setting and enforcing what they deem appropriate prices.

April 1796	Suspicions that a baker is hoarding grain to raise the price cause yet another **Food Riot**. It is quelled by Yeomanry and Dragoons. The crowd is fired upon and one person wounded, others are arrested.
May 1796	A heated **election escalates into a riot**. Following clashes with royalists, supporters of the radical candidate escort him out of town. A fierce fight in Chapel-bar ends as the royalists are routed.
April 1800.	High prices cause a **Food Riot** in which large amounts of provisions are taken. A number of people are arrested by the military and imprisoned.
August 1800	Over the course of four days, **Food Rioters** seize highly priced provisions all over town, the military being unable to stop them. Only a heavy storm can put an end to the expropriations.
1811-2 and 1816-7	These years are marked by the widespread **frame breaking by 'Luddites'** who carry out well organised armed raids in the town and the county. Specific models of frames, thought to be putting people out of work, and frames owned by hosiers cutting workers' incomes are systematically smashed. As local law enforcers are outsmarted and the practice rapidly spreads throughout the region, large numbers of soldiers are deployed. Some raids escalate, causing deaths and serious injuries on both sides. Eventually the repression succeeds. Numerous people are imprisoned, transported or hung.
May 1812	The **assassination of the Prime Minister causes jubilations** in the streets until soldiers disperse crowds.
June 1812	On-going **tensions between royalists and radicals** escalate into a riot in a theatre as the latter refuse the royalists' command to take off their hats to sing the national anthem.
June 1812	Famine causes two days of **Food Riots**. They start as a person carries a loaf on a stick over the market. One person is carried aloft by the crowd in a chair, dubbed 'Lady Ludd'. Rioters are joined by militia troops.
June 1817	An ill-fated attempt at armed insurrection, later known as the **'Pentrich rebellion'**, is swiftly ended and a number of persons executed. The uprising had been egged on and betrayed by a government agent provocateur known as 'Oliver' (who subsequently emigrated).
October 1831	Following the defeat of a very moderate parliamentary reform bill in the House of Lords, the **'Reform Riots'** erupt as large numbers of people respond with direct action to the hated 'boroughmongers' yet again succeeding in defending their privileges. Houses of known Tories, as well as dwellings and shops of their supporters and various law enforcers are attacked all over Nottingham. Crowds target the property of local grandees, such as the Fourth Duke of Newcastle. Colwick Hall is trashed, Nottingham Castle and a silk mill in Beeston burned down. An attempt to liberate prisoners from the House of Correction is thwarted by the military. Following the mobilisation of Yeomanry and large numbers of special constables, an attack on Wollaton Hall is also repelled. In the end two people are shot and wounded by the military. Three persons are subsequently hanged on the steps of Shire Hall (known today as the Galleries of Justice).

Bibliography

Local Studies Library (Nottingham Central Library)

Nottingham Journal - And Newark, Mansfield, Gainsborough, Retford, Worksop, Grantham, Chesterfield, and Sheffield General Advertiser; 8th October 1831.

Nottingham Journal...; 15th October 1831.

Nottingham Journal...; 7th January 1832.

Nottingham Journal...; 14th January 1832.

Nottingham Journal...; 21st January 1832.

Nottingham Review And General Advertiser for the Midland Counties; 30th September 1831.

Nottingham Review ...; 14th October 1831.

The Nottingham and Newark Mercury; 8th October 1831.

The ... Mercury; 15th October 1831.

Nottinghamshire Archives

DDFSI/134; *Nottinghamshire Special Assize 1832-Calendar of the Prisoners 1832.*

DD2069/1; *Compilation of commendations to 15th Hussars and South Nottinghamshire Yeomanry for their conduct during the Reform Riots.*

DD763/8; *Some Particulars of the Life, Trial, Behaviour, and execution of George Beck, George Hearson, and John Armstrong, who were Executed in Front of the County Jail, Nottingham, on Wednesday, February 1, 1832, For Burning Mr. Lowe's Mill at Beeston.*

Staveley, E./Wood, H.M.: ... *This Plan of the Town and County of the Town of Nottingham and of the several extra Parochial place within the Libertines of the Castle, together with parts of the Parishes of Lenton, Radford and Sneinton, in the County of Nottingham – From Surveys made in the Years 1827, 1828 & 1829 is dedicated with every sentiment of respect by their most obedient servants E. Staveley & H.M. Wood*; Courtesy of Nottinghamshire Archives.

University Archives (University of Nottingham)

Digitised versions of all documents (other than NeC 5026 and Nottingham Corporation...) available from UoN – Manuscripts and Special Collections (http://www.nottingham.ac.uk/manuscriptsandspecialcollections).

ChM 5/6; *Report of the proceedings against the parties charged with burning Nottingham Castle ... tried at the Special Assize holden at Nottingham, 4-14 January 1832* (retrieved 20th July 2011).

NeC 4998; *Copy letter from Dr. Alexander Manson, Nottingham, Nottinghamshire, to J. H. Barker, Mayor of Nottingham; 9 Oct. 1831*; transcribed by Kathryn Summerwill (retrieved 20th July 2011).

NeC 4999; *Letter from Thomas Winter, Red Hill, Nottinghamshire, to Henry, 4th Duke of Newcastle under Lyne; 11 Oct. 1831*; transcribed by Kathryn Summerwill (retrieved 20th July 2011).

NeC 5000; *Letter from John Sherbrooke Gell, Nottingham, Nottinghamshire, to Henry, 4th Duke of Newcastle under Lyne; 11 Oct. 1831*; transcribed by Kathryn Summerwill (retrieved 20th July 2011).

NeC 5001; *Letter from Geo. Flower, Mansfield, Nottinghamshire, to John Parkinson; 11 Oct. 1831* (retrieved 20th July 2011).

NeC 5004; *Letter from Thomas Moore, High Sheriff of Nottingham, Nottingham, to Henry, 4th Duke of Newcastle under Lyne; 12 Oct. 1831*; transcribed by Kathryn Summerwill (retrieved 20th July 2011).

NeC 5010; *Letter from Mr. J. Parkinson, Clumber Park, Nottinghamshire, to Henry, 4th Duke of Newcastle under Lyne; 12 Oct. 1831*; transcribed by Kathryn Summerwill (retrieved 20th July 2011).

NeC 5015; *Letter from Mr. W. Norton, Elton House, Nottinghamshire, to Henry, 4th Duke of Newcastle under Lyne; 14 Oct. 1831*; transcribed by Kathryn Summerwill; digitised version available from University of Nottingham – Manuscripts and Special Collections; URL see above (retrieved 20th July 2011).

NeC 5016; *Letter from Sam Parsons, Nottingham Park, Nottingham, to Henry, 4th Duke of Newcastle under Lyne; 14 Oct. 1831*; transcribed by Kathryn Summerwill (retrieved 20th July 2011).

NeC 5021; *Letter from Mr. Musters, Colwick, Nottinghamshire, to Henry, 4th Duke of Newcastle under Lyne; 16 Oct. 1831*; transcribed by Kathryn Summerwill (retrieved 20th July 2011).

NeC 5026; *An anonymous letter to the 4th Duke of Newcastle, dated Nottingham, October 19th, 1831, recounting the riots in Nottingham and the surrounding districts and complaining about the conduct of the magistrates.*

NeC 5030; *Letter from an anonymous 'Friend', Nottingham, to Henry, 4th Duke of Newcastle under Lyne; 25 Oct. 1831*; transcribed by Kathryn Summerwill (retrieved 20th July 2011).

NeC 5052; *Schedule of Prisoners committed to take their trials charged with being concerned in the riots near Nottingham on the 10th and 11th October, 1831.*

Nottingham Corporation (1833): *A report of the evidence given before the commissioners appointed to enquire into municipal corporations – Taken in short-hand by Thomas Cocayne, Reporter for the Nottingham Journal*; Nottingham Constitutional Club; Nottingham.

Published sources/Literature/Articles

1841 UK Census Collection; available from www.Ancestry.co.uk (retrieved 22nd October 2014).

BBC News (2010): *Full Text: Clegg Reform speech*; http://news.bbc.co.uk/1/hi/8691753.stm (retrieved 14th July 2011).

Beckett (a), John: ‚The Nottingham Reform Bill Riots of 1831'; in: Jones, C/Salmon, P./Davis, R.W. (2005): *Partisan Politics, Principle and Reform in Parliament and the Constituencies 1689-1880*; Edinburgh University Press; Edinburgh.

Beckett (b), John (ed./2006): A Centenary History of Nottingham; Phillimore; Chichester.

Bragg, Billy: *Electoral Reform: Be a Purple Person and make every vote count;* in: Guardian Online; http://www.guardian.co.uk/commentisfree/2010/may/10/electoral-reform-purple-person (retrieved 31st July 2010).

Braudel, Fernand (1986): *Sozialgeschichte des 15.-18. Jahrhunderts – Aufbruch zur Weltwirtschaft*; Volume 3; Kindler; München.

Bryson, Emrys (1983): *Portrait of Nottingham*; Robert Hale; London.

Clay, C.G.A. (1984): *Economic Expansion and Social Change – England 1500-1700*; Volume 2; Cambridge University Press; Cambridge.

Deering, Charles (1970): *The History of Nottingham*; S.R. Publishers; East Ardsley.

Defoe, Daniel (1986): *A Tour Through the Whole Island of Great Britain*; Penguin; London.

Dinwiddy, J.R. (1986): *From Luddism to the First Reform Bill – Reform in England 1810-1832*; Historical Association Studies; Basil Blackwell; Oxford.

Engels (a), Friedrich: ‚Über historischen Materialismus'; in: Bertram, Mathias (ed./1998): *Digitale Bibliothek Band 11: Marx/Engels – Ausgewählte Werke* (see MEW Volume 22).

Engels (b), Friedrich (2009): *The Condition of the Working Class in England*; Penguin; London.

Fellows, George/Freeman, Benson (1928): *Historical Records of the South Nottinghamshire Hussars Yeomanry 1794-1924*; Aldershot.

Field, Henry (ed./1884): *The Date Book of remarkable and memorable events connected with Nottingham and its Neighbourhood*; Vol. 2: '1750-1884'; Nottingham.

Gaunt (a), Richard A. (ed./2003): *Unhappy Reactionary: The Diaries of the Fourth Duke of Newcastle-Under-Lyne 1822-50*; Thoroton Society of Nottinghamshire; Nottingham.

Gaunt (b), Richard A. (ed.; 2010): *Politics, Law and society in Nottinghamshire: The diaries of Godfrey Tallents of Newark 1829-1839*; Nottinghamshire County Council.

Goldsmith, Oliver (1840): *The History of England – From the Invasion of Julius Caesar to the Death of George II with a Continuation to the Present Time*; Paris.

Gray, Duncan: 'Nottingham in the nineteenth century'; in: *Transactions of the Thoroton Society of Nottinghamshire*; Volume 55; Nottingham.

Hernon, Ian (2006): *Riot! Civil Insurrection from Peterloo to the Present Day*; Pluto Press; London.

Hicklin, John (1836): *The History of Nottingham Castle – From the Danish Invasion to its destruction by rioters, in 1831*; London.

Hoare, Peter: 'The operatives' libraries in Nottingham: a 19th century radical initiative; in: Blem, Askan (2001): *Festschrift fuer Peter Vodosek*; K.G. Saur; München.

Hobsbawm (a), Eric (1964): *The Age of Revolution – Europe 1789-1848*; Weidenfeld & Nicolson; London.

Hobsbawm (b), Eric (1998): *Wieviel Geschichte braucht die Zukunft;* Carl Hanser; München/Wien.

Holderness, Bryan A. (1976): *Pre-industrial England – economy and society 1500-1750;* Dent; London.

Holstun, James (2000): *Ehud's dagger: class struggle and the English Revolution;* Verso; London.

Kayne, David (1987): *The Darwen County History Series - A History of Nottinghamshire*; Phillimore; Oxford.

Le Bon, Gustave (2010): *The Crowd – A Study of the Popular Mind*; Filiquarian; Breinigsville.

Lowe, David/Richards, Jack (1982): *The City of Lace*; Nottingham Lace Centre Limited; Nottingham.

O'Brien, Jo: *Women's Liberation in Labour History – A case study from Nottingham*; Spokesman Pamphlet No. 24; Nottingham.

Pearce, Edward (2004): *Reform! The fight for the 1832 Reform Act*; Pimlico; London.

Pinchbeck, Ivy (1981): *Women Workers and the Industrial Revolution 1750-1850*; Virago; London.

Rudé, George (1967): 'English Rural and Urban Disturbances on the eve of the First Reform Bill, 1830-1831'; in: *Past & Present* 37.

Shepard, Alexandra (2000): 'Manhood, Credit, Patriarchy in Early Modern England c.1580-1640'; in: *Past & Present* 171.

'The Ten Propositions' (1647): In: Gardiner, Samuel Rawson (1951): *The Constitutional Documents of the Puritan Revolution 1625-1660*; document no. 32; Clarendon Press; Oxford.

Thirsk, Joan (1978): *Economy Policy and Projects – The Development of a Consumer Society in Early Modern England;* Oxford.

Thomis (a), Malcolm I. (1969): *Politics and Society in Nottingham 1785-1835*; Basil Blackwell; Oxford.

Thomis (b), Malcolm I. (1970): *The Luddites – Machine-Breaking in Regency England; David & Charles Archon Books*; Newton Abbot.

Thomis, Malcom I./Preston, R.A./Wigley, John: 'Nottingham and the Reform Bill Riots of 1831: New Perspectives'; in: Train, K.S.S. (1974): *Transactions of the Thoroton Society of Nottinghamshire*; Volume 77; Nottingham.

Thompson, E.P. (1980): *The Making of the English Working Class*; Victor Gollancz; London.

Trumann, Andrea (2004): ‚Das bürgerliche Subjekt und sein Anderes – Zur Subjektivierung der Geschlechtscharaktere'; in: *Phase 2 – Zeitschrift gegen die Realität* 13; S. 22-24.

Welch (a), M.A. (ed./1974): *Working Class Unrest in Nottingham 1800-1850 – Part 1 Introduction*; University of Nottingham; Nottingham.

Welch (b), M.A. (ed./1974): *Working Class Unrest in Nottingham 1800-1850 – Part 3 Reform*; University of Nottingham; Nottingham.

Wright; D.G. (1970): *Democracy and Reform 1815-1885*; Longman; London.

Wylly, H.C. (1908): *The military memoirs of Lieut.-General Sir Joseph Thackwell G.C.B., K.H.; Colonel 16th Lancers – Arranged from diaries and correspondence*; London.

Wyncoll, Peter (1985): *The Nottingham Labour Movement 1880-1939*; Lawrence and Wishart; London.